372.1302 Klavan, Ellen.
KLA
        Taming the homework
        monster.

                                    MPLD040240

$10.00

OCT 1 5 1992 DATE			
NOV 2 1 1992			

TAMING
THE
HOMEWORK
MONSTER

How to Make Homework a Positive Learning Experience for Your Child

Ellen Klavan

POSEIDON PRESS

New York London Toronto Sydney Tokyo Singapore

POSEIDON PRESS
Simon & Schuster Building
Rockefeller Center
1230 Avenue of the Americas
New York, New York 10020

POSEIDON PRESS is a registered trademark of
Simon & Schuster Inc.

POSEIDON PRESS colophon is a trademark of
Simon & Schuster Inc.

DESIGNED BY BARBARA MARKS
Manufactured in the United States of America

1   2   3   4   5   6   7   8   9   10

Library of Congress Cataloging-in-Publication Data
Klavan, Ellen.
Taming the homework monster : how to make homework
a positive learning experience for your child /
Ellen Klavan.
p.   cm.
1. Homework.   2. Study, Method of.   3. Education,
Elementary—United States—Parent
participation.   I. Title.
LB1048.K53   1992
372.13′028′1—dc20   92-17035
CIP
ISBN 0-671-74297-3

Acknowledgments

A working mother is only as good as the childcare arrangements she is able to make. I thank Linda Grant, Kelly Kenefick, Millie Perez, Lisa Redlich and Mary Wilbur—all of whom helped look after my two children at various times while I was writing this book. All are smart, caring and resourceful women who made writing this book possible.

I also heartily thank the parents and teachers who spoke candidly with me about homework monsters large and small. I thank my agent, Kris Dahl, and my editor, Ann Patty, for their guidance and attention to detail. And I thank my husband, Andrew Klavan, both for his editorial help and for his overall forbearance.

For Faith

Contents

Meeting the Monster in His Den

*P*icture a quiet suburban street. Autumn leaves are falling and swirling along the sidewalk. It's dusk and as the sunlight fades, lights are coming on in the houses. Inside many of these homes, the homework hour is upon us. If we could pass beyond the tranquil exterior of these homes and listen to what was going on inside, we'd hear . . . chaos! Parents are nagging and cajoling. Kids are whining and screaming, and several children are on the verge of tears. Before the night is over, at least one parent will be reduced to tears as well. The homework monster has been set loose upon the land!

Ask any parent you know how she feels about homework. Chances are her first reaction will be nonverbal. She may roll her eyes heavenward, grimace, and perhaps utter a short guttural grunt, a grunt that conveys . . . dismay, displeasure, possibly even despair. Ask a group of parents, as I have done, whether homework is a source of tension in their homes and nine out of ten will laugh—a little bitterly, perhaps—and ask if you're joking.

In many families, homework is a monster, a snarling beast who disrupts the evening, sets parent against child, and turns the family against the school. Children complain that homework is too hard, too boring, and too demanding. Parents complain about the quality and the quantity of their kids' homework, about the demands homework places on the entire family, about the unrealistic expectations of educators who assign homework.

In every home, the issues surrounding homework are different. In my talks with parents, I've heard about a variety of concerns. Here are a few of the most common:

✎ **My child hates homework.** "I start reminding Jack to do his homework the minute I get home from work," says Betty K. "But he just procrastinates like crazy. He does a little and then it's time for dinner. He fools around and by the time he gets around to it it's almost bedtime. He says it's too hard and he hates it but he really wastes time like crazy. It ruins our whole evening." Many children find homework tedious, hard, and basically unfun. Kids like Jack need help to learn to focus on their schoolwork and get it out of the way without procrastinating.

✎ **My child won't do her homework by herself.** "When Sally first started getting homework, she found it confusing and I used to sit with her and help her do it," says Sandra L. "Now I think she could probably handle a lot of it by herself but she insists that she can't and keeps asking for my help. If I don't help her she whines and sometimes bursts into tears." Many parents find themselves caught in Sandra's position, giving more help than they feel is appropriate. They want to help their children do well in school but they also recognize that doing the work for their kids isn't going to do anybody any good. They need to evaluate their children's skills and determine just how much help is really needed.

✎ **My child gets too much homework.** "I hate homework," says Maggie B., bravely putting into words a sentiment many parents are embarrassed about expressing. "It seems to me that when Kevin is in school six hours a day, his teacher has plenty of time to teach him what he needs to know. Now that he's in the fourth grade, he's getting almost half an hour of work a day. That's a half-hour he could spend riding his bike or playing with friends or just hanging out at home." Parents' perceptions of how much homework is the "right" amount vary widely. Maggie B. would prefer her fourth-grader had no home-work at all. Another parent I know would be delighted if her child had only a half-hour of homework a night—his teacher assigns over an hour of homework a night to third-graders!

✎ **My child doesn't get enough homework.** "Margie sits down when she gets home from school and whizzes through her homework. It's really more time-consuming than challenging. I'd like to see her get some harder assignments that really make her think," says Karen L. Ironically, Karen's child is in the same class as Kevin, the child whose mother feels he gets too much homework. When a parent feels her child isn't getting enough homework, it may well be that her child is able to do her homework more quickly and more efficiently than others in her class. In this case, the teacher may be assigning the right amount of homework for others in the class without meeting Margie's needs. Or it may be that Margie's teacher doesn't believe in assigning the amount of homework that Karen feels is appropriate.

✎ *I'm* **getting too much homework.** Laura K. says, "As soon as Reggie gets a homework assignment, it goes on *my* to-do list. I can't cross it off until he's finished. I have to keep after him until it's done. With two other children and a job, I don't have time for this extra headache." Sherry B. has fewer responsibilities than Laura but she agrees that homework takes up too much of her time. "I don't remem-ber my folks being involved with my homework all that much," she reports. "But somehow I *am* involved in Kira's work. And I don't want to do homework. I did homework already, I didn't like it, and I don't want to be doing it now."

✎ **I don't like the homework my child's teacher assigns.** This is a very common complaint, although the reasons for it vary widely. Karen L. argues, "She just gets worksheets, worksheets, worksheets. It's the same exact stuff that she does at school. It doesn't stretch her mind." But Ellen S. complains, "Sam's teacher is always assigning special projects. We have to schlep to the library to look up books about Eskimos or we have to buy art supplies to make a diorama. There's no way Sam can do these projects all by himself so I end up having to spend half the night working on them with him." Alice C. is "sick and tired" of homework assignments that are "basically arts and crafts—dioramas, posters, and so on. Whatever happened to good old-fashioned book learning?" she says. Educators differ in their perceptions of what makes for good homework and parents also have strong opinions on this subject.

✎ **My child's teacher has unreasonable expectations.** "His first week of second grade, Sam's teacher gave him a list of spelling words and told him to study it for a test on Friday," says Charlotte B. "He came home in tears—he had no idea how to go about studying for a test." Too often, teachers give assignments without giving children the tools for completing those assignments. They leave it up to the parents to impart study skills to their children.

✎ **My child is a perfectionist.** "Mary sits down very willingly when I tell her it's time to do her homework," Bill R. reports. "In fact, she's so concerned about handing in her work on time that she sometimes reminds me that it's time to get started. And she does her work very patiently. But the teacher asks the parents to check the work and Mary gets very upset when I point out her mistakes. She gets out her eraser and starts making changes and then her paper gets messy and she gets more and more upset. Sometimes she gets quite hysterical." A child like Mary, who's very concerned about doing things just right and pleasing the teacher, is probably able to control her intense emotions at school. At home, however, she feels safe enough to cry and whine if things don't come out just as she planned.

✎ **My child fights me tooth and nail.** "When I finally get Larry to sit down and get to work, he'll work for a while and then he'll say, 'I need help with this.' I'll come over and say something like, 'This is how you do it,' and he'll start to yell at me, something like 'That's not the way Mrs. Schell taught us.' And I'll get angry because, after all, he asked me for the help in the first place and soon I'm yelling and then we're yelling at each other and it gets fierce," confesses Mona R. An argument over homework can wind up becoming a full-fledged power struggle, a battle that no one can win and that certainly won't get the homework done. Often, homework is just one of many issues parents and children struggle over.

These concerns reflect the fact that each family relates to homework in a different way. If there's a homework monster in your house, he probably looks a little different from the one next door. In order to start changing the way homework is done in your house, you need to get a handle on the unique problems you're experiencing.

At some point in your child's school career, you've probably been given a list of pointers on how to supervise your child's homework. Perhaps your child's kindergarten or first-grade teacher made an announcement at her first open house. Or her school may have sent out a flyer giving you tips on handling homework. You were probably advised to set aside a particular time of day when your child would do her homework and a place where she could do it. You may have been urged to see your child's homework as her responsibility and told to supervise without becoming excessively involved in her homework.

All of which is good advice, and you probably set out to follow it faithfully when your child began bringing home homework. But you've probably had to make adjustments to meet your child's unique needs. Your child may far prefer the kitchen table, for instance, as a place for doing homework to the well-stocked, well-lighted desk upstairs in her bedroom. Sports and other after-school activities may make it impossible for your child to do her homework at the same time every night. No set of guidelines can possibly address every family's needs. Every child is different and every family fits homework into its life differently.

A recent study underscores this point. R. P. McDermott of Columbia University's Teachers College and other researchers studied the way two different families incorporated homework into their evening routines.

One family, the Kinneys, set aside a special time for Joe, a third-grader, to do his work. Joe's mother saw that his sister was occupied elsewhere and out of the way, and she sat down at the kitchen table to work with Joe. As Joe worked, his mother closely supervised him.

In the other household, the Farrells, homework took place amid the hubbub of family life. Sheila, a fourth-grader, sat at the kitchen table and did her work while other family members wandered in and out of the room. Later she brought her work to her mother to check. Sheila's mother went over her work while the baby banged on Sheila's school book, the television blared in the background, and Sheila's father put in occasional comments.

Ostensibly, Joe's mother did everything "right"—she created a quiet, private space for Joe to work in and made herself completely available to him for help and supervision. By contrast, Sheila's mother broke all the rules—she allowed her to do homework in a noisy room with the television on and gave her only partial attention as she dealt simultaneously with her baby and other people in the family.

And yet the researchers found that it was Sheila who did her homework efficiently and completely while Joe got very little work done despite his mother's efforts. While Sheila's homework fit into the ebb and flow of her family's life, Joe's mother's efforts to create a special atmosphere actually disrupted the process of doing his work. Joe and his mother spent more time talking about what they were doing, looking for a pencil, going through his backpack, and so on than they actually spent doing his homework.

"For the Farrells," the researchers conclude, "homework is not a scene apart from the rest of life, and it is not very specially organized. It is one thing to be done among a few things to be done and, if properly broken into parts, it can be fitted neatly into the flow of the day."

In the Kinney household, the researchers comment, too much attention is paid to procedures. "Attention to the eraser on his pencil, the size of his penmanship, whether a pencil or pen is used, or whether the table is clean—all these matters are often addressed at times relevant to mother and son taking on some piece of homework. Again and again they deal with the procedural matter, and they become lost on their way to the homework task."

McDermott and his colleagues aren't recommending that all children do their homework with the television on in the background while their mothers alternate watching soap operas and supervising babies with overseeing homework. But the researchers are making the point that homework has to fit into the lives of families in ways that make sense to everyone in the family. More important than following any one set of guidelines is finding the way to make homework work in your unique family.

You can start by taking a closer look at what goes on in your family. As you think about homework, think about your child as an individual. How is her schoolwork going in general? How do you and she interact when she does her homework? Think about your child's particular teacher and her particular school. Are you happy about the quality of the education she's getting? How do you feel about her homework assignments? What aspects of the homework experience are you happy with? What would you like to change?

This book won't give you a prescription for dealing with your child's homework. It will give you a framework for thinking about homework. It will give you a set of useful criteria for evaluating your child's education. And it will give you the tools you need to help your child to do homework in the way that works best for her.

PART
ONE

Whose Idea Is Homework, Anyway?

Homework has been with us a long time. Ever since colonial days, American children have been bringing home schoolwork and no doubt driving their parents crazy over it. The kinds of homework children have done, however, as well as the amount of it, has fluctuated enormously over the years. Parents' attitudes toward homework have changed as well.

A Short History of Homework

In the nineteenth century, much of elementary education consisted of rote learning. Children were taught the "Three R's" (reading, 'riting, and 'rithmetic) and weren't called upon to think creatively or to apply their school learning to the rest of their lives. Homework consisted largely of memorization. If the teacher taught multiplication tables in school that day, children memorized multiplication tables at home that night. If the children had a history lesson, they were expected to memorize the names of principal historical figures and the dates of key battles and other events.

Early in the twentieth century, educators and other social scientists began to question this method of learning. John Dewey, the preeminent educational theoretician, transformed the face of American schooling. He emphasized the importance of teaching problem-solving skills and discouraged reliance on rote memorization.

At about the same time, there was a popular outcry against homework. Proponents of the "life adjustment movement" argued that homework intruded unfairly into children's private at-home time. In 1913, the *Ladies' Home Journal* conducted a survey of administrators, doctors, and parents about the effects of homework on children. The magazine concluded that no homework whatsoever should be given to public-school students.

After World War II, this trend reversed itself. When the Russians started the "race for space" (with the launching of the Sputnik satellite in 1957) many Americans became concerned that our schoolchildren were falling behind the Russians'. Clearly we were entering a whole new, technologically sophisticated era. To keep up with our competitors, our children would need an arsenal of scientific know-how. Once again memorization came into vogue, as a means of preparing Americans for the technological battles ahead.

But then came the sixties and another ideological shift. Educators began to address the needs of the "whole child." Thinking creatively, working cooperatively and learning for the sheer joy of learning began to seem more important than being able to regurgitate a series of facts and figures. Attitudes toward homework became more relaxed. Again parents and educators became concerned about preserving children's after-school hours so that kids could play and grow in other ways besides doing schoolwork.

The last decade has seen yet another swing of the pendulum. As standardized test scores have dropped and student proficiency dwindled, a "back to basics" movement has emerged. It's all very well and good, some theorists claim, to encourage children's creativity and respect their need for recreation, but when are they going to learn to read and write? Today's parents are looking to the schools to equip their children with solid skills and practical information as well as creative problem-solving tools. Public opinion surveys have revealed that parents perceive homework as an important part of that process.

Just as Americans worried about their children's ability to compete with the Russians in the 1950s, so now Americans have begun to compare themselves with the Japanese and are finding our country lacking. The average Japanese schoolchild spends more time in school and doing homework than his American counterpart. Perhaps because of different family values, Asian-American students also score higher on standardized achievement tests than other American students.

Does that mean that we should adopt the Japanese model and make more rigorous demands on our children and our educational system? When we look at the giant strides the Japanese have made in business over the last two or three decades, it's tempting to call for a total reorganization of our educational system. But by American standards, the Japanese emphasis on cultivating children's intellectual skills neglects the development of their personal and emotional lives.

To make a valid comparison, we have to take a look at the way American children fill up the hours that aren't spent studying. If the time is spent participating in sports, playing with other children, reading for pleasure, and communicating with other family members, a case can be made that the American child has opportunities the Japanese child lacks. If, on the other hand, the American child fills up his nonstudy hours with television, junk food, and video games, the Japanese model begins to look very attractive.

As this short history of homework suggests, there is no tried-and-true formula for defining the role homework should play in children's education. The amount and type of homework assigned to elementary school students has changed enormously during this century and will probably change again in the century to come. The homework policy of your child's school represents the views of your community's educators, but it is not the last word in homework policies. Current views on the necessity and effectiveness of homework may or may not agree with your own gut-level feelings about the issue. While you—and your child—will probably have to accept prevailing attitudes about homework, it doesn't hurt to take stock of your own beliefs. If your perspective differs from the school's, you may be able to begin lobbying for a change.

Homework Rationales

Sending your child to school is the least efficient way to educate him. At school, he's one person in a large group of children with widely varying abilities. One teacher, faced with the gargantuan task of educating twenty to forty youngsters, can't possibly zero in on your child's particular educational needs. In fact the sheer administrative burden of managing those twenty to forty students—of taking attendance, of organizing them into lines for recess, of responding to their individual requests to go to the bathroom—will take up so much of her time that she'll have remarkably little time left over for educational purposes. At a school, your child has to learn to conform to a curriculum designed to educate the anonymous, generic Student— not Your Child, the individual.

Sending your child to school is, however, the most economical way to educate him. As a society—and certainly as individual families —we cannot afford to hire individual tutors and governesses for every child. If your child could have that kind of individual attention, he'd probably never need to do homework. With an individualized curriculum and personal attention from a talented educator, he could probably learn a great deal more—and in a shorter time—than his schoolbound counterpart.

Apart from being economical, schools do have other advantages. Foremost is the opportunity they provide for children to interact with one another. Especially now that families are having fewer children, the school is an important place for socialization. Not only do schools offer children the chance to play with their peers, they also teach children how to cooperate and negotiate with others—important skills that they'll need throughout their lives.

The inefficiency of schools is one of the main reasons homework exists. Half an hour of homework may not seem like all that much compared to six hours of schoolwork, but it may represent the biggest chunk of focused, purely academic work your child does all day. No matter what rationale your child's teacher uses to explain why she gives homework, the need to make up for lost school time has probably gone into the assignment.

In some cases, it's simply a matter of using fifteen minutes of homework time to work on simple drills there wasn't time to do in school. In other cases, teachers use homework as a way to assign projects that they couldn't possibly supervise in school. A big research assignment, for which each child picks his own topic, is the kind of project that is usually too much for a single teacher to handle alone.

Whether they intend to or not, most teachers rely on parents to provide the individualized attention and guidance that can't be given in school. It's a rare fourth-grader who can go to the library by himself, find the books he needs to study for a research project, go to the art supply store and pick up the materials he needs, and then come home to put together a big project by himself. Your child's teacher may encourage you to let your child work independently but she probably intends for you to give him the supervision and assistance that she can't provide at school.

Filling in the gaps that the school can't accomplish is, then, a big reason for homework. In a high-quality, well-funded school where there's a good teacher-student ratio, the gaps will be small and manageable. In a large, poorly funded school with a diverse population (which makes it harder to teach to the individual), the gaps may look more like gaping voids. How much you help your child with his homework is to some extent a function of the size of the gaps.

Here's a list of the most commonly given rationales for assigning homework. Some of these rationales are very good explanations for assigning homework; others are open to debate. When you ask your child's teacher what purpose homework serves in her classroom, she's likely to give you some of these explanations:

✎ **Homework fosters independence.** When a child is in the classroom, he is (in theory at least) working under the close scrutiny of his teacher. When he does his homework, he works on his own. As he learns to keep a list of his assignments and to budget his time so that he can do a week's assignment a little at a time, he develops the self-

Homeschooling:
Homework All the Time

For about 250,000 American children, all schoolwork takes place at home. These kids are "homeschooled," which means that their parents educate them. Homeschooling is now legal in all fifty states. Most states oversee homeschooling and children may have to take tests periodically to ensure that they are getting an education that is comparable to the one they'd be getting at local public schools. According to several studies on homeschooling, the average homeschooled student actually outperforms the average public-schooled student in every skill area.

Many of the parents who choose to homeschool their children are fundamentalist Christians who are seeking an alternative to the "godlessness" of public schools. Many others are progressive parents who believe there are better ways to educate children than through traditional educational approaches.

David and Micki Colfax educated their four children at home on the family's Boonville, California, ranch. The Colfax children spent far fewer hours sitting at their desks doing schoolwork than their traditionally educated counterparts. But, argues their father, the time they spent studying was far more focused and productive.

A description of the Colfaxes' education quoted in the *Utne Reader* is impressive: "There were no tests, set curriculums, or deadlines, but rather lots of books, field trips, educational toys, and real work on the family ranch. That work, which included projects like installing phone lines, building a guest house, and raising livestock, taught the boys intensive lessons in such areas as math, engineering, and animal sciences."

Were the Colfaxes ready for the "real world" when they finished their homeschooling education? One indication is that the three oldest children have been accepted at Harvard University. More important, however, is their parents' assessment: "Our goal in homeschooling has always been to educate our children," they write, "to facilitate the development of intellect and character— and not merely to prepare them for colleges or a career."

discipline that will serve him throughout his educational career. Of course, if teachers want to foster independence in their students, they need to give age-appropriate assignments that children really can accomplish on their own. Plus, they need to explain all new material and procedures clearly at school. When teachers do this, parents can help and support the process by refusing to become overly involved in their children's homework.

✎ **Homework reinforces skills.** This is one rationale that any nineteenth-century schoolmarm would agree with. The idea is that when children spend the day learning about forming the past tense, it helps to go home and spend the evening adding -ed to verb stems. In practice, most teachers use worksheets when they want to assign reinforcement exercises. (See "The Worksheet Debate," p. 31.)

✎ **Homework prepares the child for the next day's lessons.** Often teachers ask their students to read a particular passage or to watch the evening news or to make a list of questions in preparation for the next day's work. When children do this kind of work the night before, the day's classroom work can go into greater depth.

✎ **Homework expands the child's learning experience.** At school the child learns the bare bones of a subject; at home he can explore it more deeply and truly make it his own. For example, suppose your child's teacher has been talking about systems—the reproductive system, the sewage system, the school system, and so on. Now he's asked to go home and observe the home system. He observes the different times when the members of his family get up in the morning, how they eat breakfast, when they leave the house, when they return, and so on. Some researchers refer to this kind of homework as "extension" homework because it extends the school lesson into another context. Educators also talk about "integrative" and "creative" homework. Unlike reinforcement homework, this kind of homework calls on the child to be constructive. Often a variety of skills—reading, writing, and social studies, for example—are pulled together for a creative homework assignment.

✎ **Sometimes, homework is used as punishment.** "If you kids don't settle down, you're doing three extra math worksheets for homework tonight," screams the harried teacher. As a parent, I can really identify with the teacher who resorts to threats. (Does the sentence,

"If this room isn't cleaned up by dinnertime there'll be no TV this evening!" sound familiar to you?) However, using homework as a punishment is obviously a mistake. Kids already tend to have pretty negative feelings about homework—using homework as a punishment will turn them off even more.

✎ **Homework enhances parent-school communication.** Although experts disagree on how much direct input parents should have in their children's homework, there is strong evidence linking parental involvement in children's schoolwork with higher scholastic performance. Many teachers see homework as a way of keeping parents abreast of what's happening in school. By looking over my second-grader's shoulder occasionally, for example, I know that borrowing and carrying are now part of her repertoire of math skills, that she's learning about consonant blends and homonyms and that she's studying the Algonquin Indians. When parents are aware of what their children are doing in school, they can informally reinforce the lessons their children are learning. Homework as a means of parent-school communication can go the other way, too. Many teachers report that parents raise concerns about the school curriculum based on the assignments they see coming home. In many cases, teachers respond to parental pressure to give more homework.

Yes, but Does It Work?

Whatever your attitude about homework, chances are you can find a scholarly study to back you up. To date, about a hundred research projects have analyzed homework's effectiveness. The results of these studies have ranged from enthusiastic endorsements of homework to calls for decreasing students' homework load on the grounds that homework has little if any impact on student achievement.

In the last decade, several scholars have conducted independent reviews of the literature on homework. Each of these contemporary scholars has come away with the discouraging report that the previous studies are so riddled with methodological faults that they can only be read as highly flawed guideposts at best. The definitive study on homework effectiveness has yet to be written.

Harris Cooper, a research associate and professor of psychology at the University of Missouri Center for Research in Social Behavior, has conducted what is probably the most thorough and exhaustive survey of homework research. He finds that, overall, the research endorses homework as a useful adjunct to learning. "The average student doing more homework outperforms about 65% of students doing less homework," Cooper reports in his book *Homework*.

However, Cooper points out that many of the homework studies lump together children in all or several grade levels. Homework is most useful, Cooper reports, in high school and least useful in elementary school.

"It appears that the effect of homework on the achievement of high school students is impressive," Cooper writes. "Relative to (a) other instructional techniques, (b) the associated research and synthesis methods and (c) the costs involved in its implementation, homework can produce a substantial positive effect on adolescents' performance in school. For young children the effect may be small, even bordering on trivial."

This is disheartening news for those of us who have been agonizing with our children over their weekly spelling lists. It's worth remembering, however, that virtually all the research is, by Cooper's own description, suspect. Just because research hasn't found a positive link between homework and elementary school achievement doesn't mean that one doesn't exist.

Despite a few dissenting voices, the community of elementary school educators is on the whole united in its view that homework is indeed constructive. In 1986, the United States Department of Education produced a publication called *What Works*, designed to help parents and teachers ensure that American schoolchildren get the best education possible. The publication, which has been enormously influential, comes down squarely in favor of homework. Unlike Harris Cooper, *What Works* interprets the research as supporting the value of doing homework in all grades. "Student achievement rises significantly when teachers regularly assign homework and students conscientiously do it," the publication asserts. "Extra studying helps children at all levels of ability."

Even Harris Cooper, who finds homework relatively unimportant as a means of boosting elementary school achievement, nevertheless sees homework as valuable. He says that in early elementary school, "students can be given homework assignments meant not so much to foster achievement as to promote good attitudes and good study habits, to expel the notion that learning occurs only in school, and to allow parents the opportunity to express to their children how much they value education."

In any case, the chances are that your child's teacher regards homework as an inevitable part of his education. In all likelihood, your child will get increasingly large amounts of homework throughout his elementary school years. Whether that homework proves constructive and useful or turns out to be merely pointless drudgery depends to a large extent on the kind of homework his teacher assigns.

What's the "Right" Homework Assignment?

Not surprisingly, educators offer different recipes for the ideal homework stew. In some communities, schools mandate homework policies that teachers must adhere to. Other communities leave assigning homework up to the individual teacher. Here are some of the hallmarks of a solid, beneficial approach to homework:

✎ **Children should receive *reasonable* amounts of homework.** Some educators suggest that teachers assign ten minutes of homework per grade level. First graders would receive ten minutes of homework, for instance, while sixth graders would work for an hour each night. Other educators are more moderate. Harris Cooper, for example, suggests one to three mandatory assignments per week, each lasting no more than fifteen minutes, for students in grades one through three, and two to four mandatory assignments per week, each lasting fifteen to forty-five minutes, for students in grades four to six.

In some classrooms, children have the opportunity to start their homework at school, so an assignment that takes thirty minutes altogether may only take ten or fifteen at home. Some teachers also send home uncompleted classwork as additional homework. So two children in the same class may bring home very different amounts of homework. Whatever the teacher's policy, your child should not have to bring home more work than he can handle.

✎ **Homework should be manageable.** Homework assignments should be based on skills children have already acquired in school. A good assignment shouldn't be so easy that it's boring but neither

The Worksheet Debate

At some point in his educational career, your child will almost certainly start bringing home worksheets. The subject of a fairly heated educational debate, worksheets are used both in the classroom and as homework, as a convenient way to reinforce basic skills. In many cases, these worksheets have been produced by the same publishers who produce readers and other textbooks. Sometimes the teacher herself draws up a worksheet that applies directly to the week's lessons.

On the pro side, educators argue that worksheets offer a simple, straightforward method of drilling students. As one teacher says, "There's no substitute for practice." A certain amount of information, this argument goes, just has to be committed to memory, and worksheets facilitate rote learning. Furthermore, commercially prepared worksheets ease the burden of overworked teachers, freeing them up to concentrate on teaching.

On the con side are critics who complain that repetitive exercises are so dull that they turn kids off. When kids who receive a lot of worksheets complain that their homework is "boring," they may have a pretty good point. In the case of reading-related worksheets, some educators argue that an approach that segregates one particular skill—recognizing past participles, for example—from the rest of reading keeps children from taking in the big picture of language arts.

Your child will probably have to put up with a certain number of worksheets as a fact of life but if his homework consists entirely of worksheets, you'll be within your rights to bring your concerns to the teacher.

should it be so challenging that the child feels defeated. Children need to feel good about their ability to complete homework assignments. Short-term assignments are generally more manageable for elementary school—age children than long-term assignments. A week-long assignment is the most a child in the first through fourth grades can generally be expected to handle. If a teacher assigns a week-long assignment, like an essay, for example, she should spell out for the child how the work should be done. For example, the teacher might tell the child to gather information on Monday, write a draft on Tuesday, edit the draft on Wednesday and then write the final copy on Thursday.

✎ **Homework should not be busywork.** If your child's homework consists entirely of commercially produced worksheets, her teacher isn't working very hard on the assignments. Assignments should tie into the work your child is doing in class. While there's bound to be some mechanical work (working through a series of math problems, for example), there should be some creative work (using spelling words in an essay, for example) as well.

✎ **Homework should include reading.** Reading is arguably the most important skill your child will learn in elementary school, since it is a tool he will use in all his other subjects as well. In kindergarten and first grade, the teacher may ask you to read to your child. Later, the teacher may ask your child to read for a certain period of time each night or to read a particular passage in the class reader.

✎ **Homework should be mandatory.** Homework is most effective when all the children in the class receive the same or similar assignments. The teacher may offer additional voluntary work as well. When a class is very heterogeneous, the teacher may individualize assignments so that each student is challenged at his own level. Individualized assignments may backfire, however, as they draw children's attention to the differences in their skills. Clever teachers give open-ended assignments that each child can carry out to the best of his ability.

✎ **Children should receive feedback on their homework.** When children work hard at their homework, hand it in, and then never see it again, it's hard for them to understand that there's a point or purpose to doing homework. The homework need not be graded—

Homework in a Technological Age

The technological revolution is already having an effect on the way homework is done across the country. Here are just a few recent innovations:

   ✎ **Homework hotlines.** Throughout the country, homework hotlines are available to help kids negotiate thorny homework assignments. Kids call up and reach retired teachers and other volunteers who advise them about their homework.

   ✎ **Homework on TV.** Kids in Duval County, Florida, can tune in to homework assistance three nights a week. Weekly programs aired on WJCT-TV, a public education station, are "Hotline Math," "It's Up to Me," and "Hotline Science." Kids call in their homework questions and teachers show them how to find the answers on the air. There are similar programs in Chicago, Illinois; Fairfax, Virginia; and Sacramento, California.

   ✎ **Voice mail.** Parents of students at Los Naranjos Elementary School in Irvine, California, can call the school any night to find out about their kids' homework assignments. They call the school, enter a touch tone code, and listen to a message from the teacher.

some educators argue against grading homework—but the child's effort should be acknowledged. The sooner the child receives feedback from the teacher, the better. Furthermore, the teacher should do more than merely acknowledge that the assignment has been completed. She should look over your child's work and note any problem areas.

Feedback at home is important too. When your child brings home his corrected homework (and other schoolwork), take the time to look over it with him and praise him. Try not to be critical when you look over his work; rather, praise him for his efforts.

The Future of Homework

If the history of homework in the past century is any indication, we can expect new attitudes and new approaches to emerge in the decades ahead. The nature of work of all kinds is undergoing a transformation as information technology burgeons. For the first time in history, a stockbroker can trade shares on Wall Street from the computer in his Vermont farmhouse. Computers, telephones, and videocassettes have created myriad new possibilities for working and learning.

Many upper-middle-class families now include a computer in their list of essential appliances. Many more families own VCRs. And of course just about every American family owns a television and a telephone. The National Education Association, in its research guide to homework, predicts: "As we look forward to an age of videodiscs and cassettes, home computers, and new possibilities for educational TV through cable networks and satellite transmission, it appears obvious that we are on the brink of an era of unprecedented growth of home study."

Just as more and more professionals are leaving the conventional workplace to set up shop in their dens or living rooms, so students may begin to spend less time at school and more time working from home. For most families, though, the age of homework via telecommunications sounds more like science fiction than reality. The current generation of schoolchildren will probably continue to carry home handwritten spelling tests and photocopied math problems for the duration of their elementary school careers.

TWO

Tapping the Source: The School and Its Agenda

Your child's homework doesn't spontaneously generate itself in her backpack while she's walking home from school each afternoon. It originates at school, where it springs from a general educational philosophy as well as a particular curriculum.

In order to understand fully what your child's homework is all about you need to know what the school expects of her. The more you know about her school, its educational philosophy, and its teaching practices, the more you'll understand about where homework fits into the process.

How Good Is Your Child's School?

When you're confident that your child is attending an excellent school with a good reputation, you can probably trust that her homework has an appropriate role in her education. You'll probably feel comfortable sitting back and letting the school educate your child. If there are problems with the school, however, you may discover that you need to take a more personal role in your child's education.

If you can afford to pay for private school tuition or if you live in a community where parents are allowed to select the public school their children attend, then you have experienced the luxury of choice. You're probably reasonably happy with the quality of education your child is receiving and if you're not you're probably considering a change.

But if you're like the majority of parents, your choice is limited to the public school in your neighborhood. And the sad fact is that public education is far from perfect. Cutbacks in funding have left gaping holes in many children's educations. And the exodus of talented female and minority teachers who have left a once-prestigious occupation to find more money and respect elsewhere has shrunk the pool of top-notch educators. Standardized tests are an imperfect way of evaluating student achievement but the fact that scores are steadily declining speaks poorly for American education.

It makes sense to be realistic about your child's school. Gene I. Maeroff, author of *The School-Smart Parent* (Henry Holt), suggests these criteria (among others) for evaluating your child's school:

✎ **Expenditures.** Schools vary widely in the amount of money they spend per student. In Alaska, for instance, the average amount spent per student is $8,842, while in Utah the average expenditure is $2,455. Money spent translates into teacher salaries, up-to-date equipment, enrichment programs, and other features that make for an excellent education.

✎ **Facilities.** Do the children have plenty of room to study and play in a safe environment? How well-stocked or spacious are the library, the gym, the outdoor areas?

✎ **School climate.** When you visit the school, is it run in an orderly manner? Do both teachers and students keep their voices at a reasonably low level? Is it a place where you would like to spend six hours a day?

✎ **Class size.** An ideal student-teacher ratio (rarely reached) is fewer than twenty students per teacher, especially in the lower grades. If there are thirty or more students in your child's class, it will be almost impossible for her to receive individualized attention.

✎ **Student-teacher interaction.** The teacher should be supportive of the children, praising them frequently. She should also be able to set and maintain appropriate limits so that the class never runs wild. She should know each child's individual personality and abilities. The children should be cheerful and enthusiastic.

If your child attends a good school, she'll be learning all the time. At the end of each school year, she'll know a lot more than she did at the beginning of the year. She'll be reading more sophisticated books, will have acquired new math skills, and will share with you her new knowledge of social studies, science and other subjects.

The School Homework Policy

How does homework fit into the curriculum at your child's school? A good way to start answering this question is to find out whether the school has a homework policy. Ask your child's teacher, the head of the PTA, or the school principal for a copy of the school's homework policy.

Homework policies vary widely from school to school, even within the same school district. A good policy will describe the purpose of homework, the type of homework that will be given at each grade level and the amount of time it should take students to complete their work. It will also clarify the roles of teacher, parent and student.

Not every school has a schoolwide homework policy, and some educators oppose the idea, arguing that these policies undermine the teacher's autonomy. For example, Elvira Travis, principal of Slowe Elementary School in Washington, D.C., argues, "I don't believe in requiring homework because I think it is an integral part of classroom work. How homework is scheduled should be up to the teacher. The teacher can best determine when the children's progress, or lack of it, calls for extra preparation."

For parents, on the other hand, a homework policy is a useful guide to understanding what the school expects of the child. Your child's school may have an informal, nonwritten homework policy, a sophisticated plan, or no policy at all. If there is no policy at your child's school, you may want to suggest that the school develop one.

A Sample Homework Policy

Here are relevant portions of a well-crafted, useful policy, developed by the San Bruno Park Elementary School District in San Bruno, California:

The objective of homework is to assist and improve a student's learning. Homework is to be reasonable in length, directly related to classroom work, well defined in advance by the teacher, understood by the student, corrected and returned to the student, and non-punitive.

It is the student's responsibility to complete homework. It is the parent's responsibility to support this portion of the educational program by encouragement and involvement with the student.

The types of homework assignments and length should vary according to the student's level:

1. *Kindergarten* (Minimal, as needed)
   Homework *is to be minimal* and based on teacher judgment of the student's needs.
2. *Primary grades: 1–3* (15 to 30 minutes, as needed)
   a. Homework *is to be started* as an expectation in the student's educational program.
   b. Homework is assigned at the discretion of the teacher with an emphasis on reading, math and language arts.
3. *Middle grades: 4–6* (30 minutes to 1 hour, as needed)
   a. Homework *is to be expected* as part of the student's educational program.
   b. Homework emphasis is on reading, math and language arts.
   c. Additional assignments are given which, in the judgment of the teacher, will assist the student to learn and develop initiative and responsibility.

What to Do If You Disagree with the School's Homework Policy

If you disagree with the school's homework policy, the first person you should talk to is your class PTA representative. Through her, you may want to go to the president of the PTA as well. The PTA exists precisely to mediate concerns like these, and you will probably find that the people you talk to are happy to hear from you. Tell them what's on your mind and find out how they feel about the homework policy.

If you discover that the majority of parents approve of the homework policy, it's very unlikely that you'll be able to effect a change. If, however, a good number of parents agree with you (or at least the minority of parents who are vocal and assertive in expressing their concerns), you may be able to make a change.

Your next step might be to approach some of the teachers in the school and solicit their informal, "off the record" opinion of the policy. If they too seem to think the policy is wrong, then you're in good shape to address the school principal.

Nobody likes to be ganged up on. Don't show up at the principal's door with a vigilante mob of angry parents, waving a petition and demanding a change. Instead, go through the PTA. Urge the president of the PTA to schedule an appointment to talk to the principal. Or the PTA might write a letter, outlining its concerns and proposing an alternative policy. Through a series of meetings and discussions, you may well be able to effect a change.

" I am tired of teaching and testing our ten-year-old son on punctuation rules—'He's just going to have to memorize them,' I was told one evening after a particularly difficult time with a distraught child who had worked diligently on previous homework assignments, but just wasn't remembering the number of the rule that applied in a given spot; but then most of us don't either, I thought. I would rather spend time with them making popcorn . . . but we just don't have the time most days.

"I am tired of chivying on a child to get the spelling assignment done. I am tired of assignments that require the identification of a word without needing to understand its meaning. I would rather spend time with them playing ball or Yahtzee . . . but we don't have time most days.

"I am tired of checking material for a rote memorization social studies test. I would rather spend time talking with them about anything under the sun or snuggled up where it's warm, reading the next chapter in *The Western Game,* a book that has been renewed three times, testimony to the rareness of sharing books together . . . but we don't have the time most days."

—KATHARINE SAMWAY, writing in *Language Arts*

The Teacher's Policy

Whether your child's school has a homework policy or not, a good deal of discretion is probably left to the teacher. It's very important, then, that you find out what she expects of you and your child.

At the beginning of the school year, there's probably an open house or a back-to-school night. Many teachers take this opportunity to address parents about homework. If the teacher doesn't talk about homework, by all means raise your hand (you're in her classroom, remember) and ask. It's a good idea to raise the subject in this particular context because there will be other parents there who'll hear her answer too; if there are problems later on, you may be glad they were there.

If there is no open house or back-to-school night, seek out your child's teacher and ask her about her personal homework policy. If you are able to go to your child's school, you might talk to the teacher before or after school. Or you can call the school and leave a message for her to call you back. You might talk with the teacher over the phone or arrange to have a conference with her.

Most teachers are glad to hear from parents—the lack of parental involvement is a frequent complaint among educators. If your child's teacher doesn't return your phone calls and seems unwilling to talk with you, don't hesitate to get in touch with the principal or another administrator at the school. You'll want to approach this process tactfully, however. (See "What to Do If You Disagree with the Teacher's Policy," p. 42.)

Some of the questions you should ask your child's teacher are:

1. What kinds of homework do you assign?
2. How much time each night (or each week) should my child spend on homework?
3. What should I do if the homework takes longer (or shorter) than that?
4. Do you feel that I should be involved in the homework process, and if so, in what ways?

The fourth question is the tricky one, and you want to make sure you pin down a clear response from your child's teacher. Teachers have widely diverging attitudes about parental involvement in homework. Your child's teacher may have any of these responses:

✎ **"Homework is entirely your child's responsibility and you should have nothing to do with it."** If she says this, ask her what she expects you to do when your child says she can't do a particular assignment. And ask her what she will do if an assignment comes back half-completed or with wrong answers.

✎ **"I'd like you to check her homework after she does it herself."** This approach assumes that your child can do her homework on her own but calls on you to make sure it has been done properly. Ask the teacher exactly what she means by "checking." Does she want you simply to see that the assignment has been completed—all the questions answered, for example—but not to comment at all on the quality of the work? Or does she want you to go over the homework and point out the errors? Does she want you to correct the errors yourself or send your child back to rework those questions?

✎ **"I'd like you to work with your child on her homework."** Many teachers, particularly those with limited resources and large classes, actively solicit parent involvement in the homework process. Your child's teacher may want you to help her memorize spelling words and math facts, give pretests (in which you quiz your child on the material that will be on the next day's test), and talk over essay assignments. This approach may be particularly common in a school where overall test scores are low and teachers are anxious to do everything they can to upgrade the quality of their students' work.

What to Do If You Disagree with the Teacher's Policy

If you disagree with your child's teacher's policy, you have three choices. You can live with it, you can try to change it, or you can ignore it.

Sometimes the wisest course is simply to go along with the teacher's approach, even if you would do things differently if you were in her shoes. After all, your child has to function in an environment the teacher has created; it may be best for her that you fulfill the role the teacher has described for you. Unlike the school homework policy, which affects all seven years your child spends in elementary school, the teacher's policy will only affect your child for one year. Instead of "making a scene"—something your child probably dreads—you might just live with the teacher's policy for a year.

If the teacher's approach to homework deeply offends you, you might schedule a conference to talk it over with her and explain your objections. Chapter 4 gives suggestions for effective parent-teacher communication. If the teacher's approach differs from the school's general homework policy, you'll have a strong position from which to argue. Make sure that you approach the teacher in a respectful, collaborative spirit.

If you can't get the teacher to change and you find her policy impossible to live with or to ignore, you may want to consider appealing to a higher authority. Be careful about doing this, though. You don't want to antagonize your child's teacher by going over her head to her boss. Then too, the principal is likely to support her staff's policies and decisions. On the other hand, the teacher may take your concerns more seriously when you go to the principal about them.

The best strategy may be to talk with your class PTA representative and enlist her help in interceding with the principal. If the school has a written homework policy and the teacher's assignments are clearly contrary to the spirit of the policy, you'll be able to make a pretty strong case to the principal. If your complaint is more intangible, you'll be on shakier ground.

If you can't live with the teacher's policy but don't want to debate it with her, you might choose to ignore it. She's not *your* teacher; unlike your child, you don't have to do whatever she says. If your child isn't getting any help from the teacher when she returns half-completed assignments and her grades are slipping, you may feel compelled to get more involved in her homework, despite the teacher's "hands-off" policy. If working with your child on her homework is generating major fights between the two of you, you may feel it's not worth it to work with your child, regardless of the teacher's expectation that you do so. If your child's teacher is generally helpful and supportive, you might try talking with her and explaining that her policy, though it may be a good one, isn't working for you and your child.

"The school *and* the teacher had said, 'Don't help your child with the homework, we want to know how she's doing.' But Sophie was bringing home math homework and would look at it and be baffled. She was totally frustrated because she was not sure what she was doing and she'd cry and get more frustrated. I realized that she didn't have a clue as to how to do the assignment and I'd have to teach her what she didn't know, which was tricky for me because I didn't know how she was being taught.

"I went to her teacher but the teacher was vague. Her attitude was that everything was okay. So then I made an appointment to see the head of the lower school and I asked my ex-wife (with whom I share custody of Sophie) to join us. The head of the lower school listened carefully, and promised that she'd observe the math period of the class and talk to the teacher about Sophie's progress. They agreed to give Sophie more attention, and also I got more clarification from the teacher about what she should be learning.

"I continued to sit with Sophie and help her with her math problems. She was learning how to do the math while she did her homework. At the same time she got extra attention in school. Once it became something she could understand she started to enjoy it."

—ROBERT W.

As you evaluate your own relationship to the homework process, think about the quality of education your child is receiving. If she hasn't been taught study skills at school, it will be up to you to teach them at home. If she hasn't grasped a particular concept in the class-room, it may be up to you to help her get a handle on it. If, on the other hand, the teacher has adequately prepared her to face tonight's homework, she may need you to support her independent efforts to tackle the work alone.

THREE

At Home: Setting the Stage

S ome of the most effective strategies for taming the home-work monster are also the simplest. They involve organizing your household to make room for your child to accomplish his homework task.

Do you remember your first job? Everything was new to you—there was so much to learn! Things that are second nature to you now —putting one caller on hold while you talk to another, sending a copy of a business letter to an interested third party, developing and using a file system, for example—were novel techniques that you had to learn and incorporate into your daily routine. If you were lucky enough to work for a supportive supervisor, you had a teacher who understood that it takes time to learn how to function effectively in a work environment.

In a way, homework is your child's first job. It's the first time he's been expected to carry out an assignment independently and have it ready, by a certain deadline, for the "boss" to see. Since he's never worked before, he hasn't had a chance to develop the work habits that will stand him in good stead later in life. As you help him to organize his homework, you train him not only for years of doing homework but also for performing "real" jobs when he grows up.

When they assign homework, teachers rarely take the time to explain to children how to go about doing it. It's up to you to create a conducive work environment for your child and to teach him how to organize and carry out his assignments.

The time you spend helping your child learn to be organized will be well spent. Stop and think about the role organization plays in your own life. If you keep a running list of the supplies you need and take it with you when you go to the shopping center, you won't have to make three or four extra, time-consuming trips throughout the week. By the same token, the child whose homework is well organized can spend less time working and more time playing.

If yours is the kind of household where scissors are always kept in a certain drawer, dinner is always on the table at 6:30 and the children are in their beds by 8:15, it will probably be relatively easy for you to incorporate homework into your family's routine. If you're like the rest of us, you'll have to work a little harder to ensure that your child has the right environment to do his work.

As you think about helping your child organize his homework, remember the example, given earlier, of the child who did her homework successfully in a comparatively chaotic environment. Don't try to rearrange your lives utterly—it's too big a project and probably won't work out. Instead, think about ways to fit homework into your present life-style.

"In public school, Jane had homework problems in the fifth and sixth grades. She didn't understand what was expected of her and she was afraid to ask. I told her, 'You must tell us when you're having a test, so we can help you study.' So one day she said, 'We're having a test.' So we said, 'Okay, what's it on?' The teacher had said something like, 'Tomorrow we're having a test on this topic and this topic and this topic.' Jane had written all that down and was studying the list of topics. She didn't understand that she was supposed to get out her book and read about those topics.

They never taught her how to study. This year she's going to a Catholic school and things are going much better."

—JOAN McM.

Homework enters your family's life a little at a time and it makes different demands on you as time goes on. I've broken up the next section of tips according to your child's grade level. As I've mentioned, the kind and amount of homework that teachers assign varies widely, so you may find that the advice I give for fourth-graders applies to your second-grader, or vice versa.

Kindergarten

Your child probably won't receive homework in kindergarten. If he does, it will probably consist of occasional, fun assignments designed to get your child used to doing homework. Practice homework is a good idea, one that you can institute even if your child's teacher doesn't.

✎ **Stage a homework rehearsal.** To get your child used to the idea of doing homework, consider setting aside a short time—five to ten minutes, for example, each afternoon or evening—that you spend on "homework." If your child is beginning to read, you could look at simple storybooks together and help your child sound out the words. You could ask him to practice his letters. Or you could ask him to draw a picture or dictate a story to you. You might read him a book and then talk about it together. These homework rehearsals should be fun for your child. Don't expect him to work independently unless he wants to. You won't "spoil" him by spending this time with him. You'll just give him the idea that homework is part of life.

First through Third Grades

Sometime after kindergarten, homework will begin in earnest. It's time to start reorganizing your afternoons or evenings.

✎ **Decide on a place to do homework.** It's a good idea to designate one place in the house as the place where your child consistently does his homework. That place may or may not be his room. If your child is very independent or if you live in a small apartment where your child's room is close to the main activity of the household, he may be happy to work at his own desk in his own room. In most cases, though, young children prefer to be close to their parents when they do their homework.

Among the families I've spoken to, the kitchen table is almost universally the preferred place for doing homework. Typically, the child sits at the table and does his work while Mom or Dad makes dinner or, if homework takes place after dinner, washes up the dishes. This arrangement can work out quite well. By staying nearby but busy, you make it clear that you're available to supervise but don't intend to devote your full attention to your child's homework. Psychologically, this is a good approach to take, especially with a younger child.

Letting your child work at the kitchen (or dining room) table can create logistical problems, though, especially when you need to set the table but your child's only halfway through his math worksheet. Or when the baby's crying and you don't have time to clear the table so your child can get to work. If you have the space in your kitchen or nearby dining room, you might consider setting up a little desk for your child. If that's not possible you'll just have to time your child's use of the table so that it doesn't conflict with the table's other purposes.

Your child may come up with some other "ideal" spot for doing homework, such as the living-room sofa with a lapboard. Don't be too rigid about where he does the work, as long as the work gets done.

Don't be too concerned either about the way your child sits while he works. It can be irksome to see a child's body splayed out over the dining room table but if he's getting the work done, avoid lecturing him about his posture. Reading, in particular, should be done in any position that feels comfortable. If your child likes to lie on the living room rug with his feet on the family dog's back while he reads, leave him alone!

✎ **Create a homework shelf.** Has your office ever moved? If so, you know what it feels like to try to conduct business while your important papers are in four different boxes and your new desk hasn't arrived yet. Whatever kind of job you do, you probably have certain equipment—whether it's computer disks, a Rolodex, surgical equipment, or crescent wrenches—that you depend upon to perform your job properly. You need to know where that equipment is at all times and you need to have a well-organized place to work.

Somewhere in the house, preferably somewhere near the place where your child does his homework, designate a shelf to be used exclusively for work that travels back and forth from school. When he gets home from school, he should get into the habit of taking his homework out of his backpack (or book bag or whatever he uses to carry supplies to and from school) and putting it on this shelf. If that's too much to handle, he could just leave the backpack itself on the shelf. Here are some of the things that should be kept on this shelf:

- Any books that he's reading on a nightly or ongoing basis as part of his homework
- Any folders, books, or supplies that only go to school on certain days
- School library books
- Musical instruments, sheet music, and other supplies relating to after-school music lessons
- The sticker book, baseball cards, or other collectibles that he "has to" bring to school on a regular basis
- A basket of supplies (see the box on p. 52)

Ideally, this system will eliminate from your lives the phrase "Mom, where's my science folder?" which is generally uttered two minutes before the school bus is due to arrive.

Just as important as the things that go on your child's homework shelf are the things that should *not* be on the shelf, for example:

- Half-completed art projects
- Baseball mitts that need to be resewn
- Piles of outdated school notices
- Returned homework papers

When your child finishes his homework, ask him to pack it up, along with anything else he may need tomorrow (the science folder, for example) in his backpack and leave the backpack either on the homework shelf or at some other designated location. (Next to the front door is a good spot.)

✎ **Make a homework schedule.** Your child will need a block of time, each afternoon or evening, when he can work on his homework. It needn't be the same time each day but it's usually best if you plan in advance when your child will do his homework. If you don't, it's likely to get pushed to the end of the day, when your child is tired, which is generally the worst time to do homework. It's also the time of day when you have the least leverage. "Get your homework done so you can play outside before it gets dark," is a whole lot more effective than "Get your homework done so you can go to bed!"

If you and your spouse both work away from home in the afternoon, your child is probably in some form of after-school care. If his after-school activities involve sports or other organized activities, homework will have to wait until he gets home. If his after-school care is conducive to doing homework, you may want to suggest that he do at least some of his homework there so that his (and your) evenings will be less hectic. If you do this, check on his homework periodically to make sure he is completing it in what you consider a satisfactory manner.

If one parent is home in the afternoon, you may want to ask your child to do his homework when he gets home from school. Getting homework done before dinner leaves the evening free for play and family time. But most kids need a little transition time to wind down after school. You may want to give him a snack and let him play outdoors for an hour or so before he does his homework.

These days, homework has a lot of competition. Many kids are involved in after-school activities including sports, music, and crafts, whether their parents are working or not. And of course children need to socialize with their classmates, so many afternoons are taken up with play dates. In the evening there are baths to be taken, dinners to be eaten, favorite TV shows to be watched, books to be read, and time to be spent with the whole family.

Nevertheless, it's important to carve out a distinct period of time that will be devoted exclusively to homework. Sit down with your child and make up a schedule outlining the times each day of the week that he will spend doing homework. If something special is happening on a given week—a piano recital, for instance, or a visit from a relative or a performance of the school play—discuss at the beginning of the week how you are going to work homework into your child's schedule.

If your child has trouble focusing on his homework for a sustained period of time, you might consider breaking up the time. He could do ten minutes of homework, break for ten minutes and then come back and finish it up. This is better than letting him dawdle and procrastinate during a single longer time period. Depending on his style, you might also suggest that he switch back and forth among subjects—he could do half his language arts worksheet and half his math problems, then take a break and finish up. That way each piece of homework will be smaller and more manageable.

✎ **Offer a snack.** It's hard to work when you're hungry. Younger children in particular find food comforting and all children enjoy eating, so having a snack makes homework more enjoyable. If your child is especially active and has trouble concentrating, eating while he works may help him by keeping his hands and mouth busy.

"Marissa's getting about twenty minutes of homework a night, four nights a week, now that she's in third grade. The teacher gives out the homework at the beginning of the week and tells what day each part of it is due. Mondays and Wednesdays, Marissa has after-school, and by the time we get home it's really a drag fitting homework in along with everything else. Tuesdays and Thursdays I get off work early and pick her up from school. So those afternoons we have more time and she does most of her homework then. Like on Tuesday she does the homework that's due on Wednesday and on Thursday. Thursday she does her homework that's due Friday, which usually includes doing a long project, like writing sentences. She does the most homework on Tuesday. We come home and Marissa has a snack. Then she does about twenty minutes of homework. She has her bath, watches a half-hour of television, and then does another twenty minutes or so of homework before dinner. Maybe it would be better if she did the same amount of homework each night, but this works for us."

—KATHY G.

Supply and Demand

Homework sessions go a lot more smoothly when they don't begin with a mad hunt all over the house for a pencil with an intact eraser at its end. Make a basket of supplies for your child. A rectangular container big enough for papers to lie flat in is best. Clear plastic makes it easier to find the supplies your child needs. By all means take you child shopping at the beginning of the year and let him pick out the supplies he wants.

I suggest giving your child plenty of supplies because, in the first place, everyone knows these things get eaten by household spirits. And, more important, having plenty of work supplies makes a person feel powerful. Imagine sitting at your own desk and opening the center drawer to find one stubby pencil and a chewed-up pen. Now imagine opening the drawer to find a neat tray filled with newly sharpened pencils, capped pens, a little dish of paper clips, and a box of rubber bands. You see what I mean.

Your child's homework supply basket should contain:

- Six to ten pencils (Ask your child's teacher what size is best for him at this stage of development.)
- A pencil sharpener (Or install an electric sharpener for the whole family's use somewhere near your child's work space. They're much easier and more fun to use, and create sharp, highly satisfying points.)
- Two or three erasers
- A set of colored markers
- Scissors
- A ruler (one that shows both inches and centimeters)
- A stapler and staples
- Tape
- Twenty to thirty sheets of wide-ruled writing paper (the kind used in his school)
- Twenty to thirty sheets of plain white paper
- A folder to keep the lined and plain paper "fresh"
- Paper clips

When your child is done with his homework, teach him to *put all his supplies back in the basket!*

✎ **Turn off the TV!** *Some* TV viewing is a fact of life in most American households. (It certainly is in mine.) You don't need me to tell you how bad *excessive* TV viewing can be for your child. Studies have linked TV viewing to passivity, obesity, violent behavior, sexism, and racism in children.

One of the advantages of homework is that it takes up time that might otherwise be spent watching TV. The TV should not be on when your child is doing his homework. It's too much of a distraction. If you're in the habit of watching the news while you make dinner, don't invite your child to do his homework in the kitchen while you cook. Or change your habit.

Listening to the radio or stereo while he works, however, may be all right. Some children find the rhythm of music—even rock music —helps them to work. Others find it too distracting. Before you rule the radio out, observe your child and see how it is affecting his work habits. If he's goofing off, singing along with his favorite records, eliminate the music. If you find that he works while he listens, consider allowing the radio or stereo. Insist that he keep the volume reasonably low, and don't let him listen to talk shows while he works.

✎ **Minimize distractions.** You don't have to turn your home into a mausoleum to provide a conducive atmosphere for your child to work in. He's used to working in school where even under the best of circumstances there's usually a lot of bustle and noise. But try to shield him from particularly tempting distractions. Don't get into any interesting arguments with his younger brother, for example, or make a dreaded dental appointment over the phone while he's nearby.

Many people assume that children should study alone, but that's not necessarily true. If your child and his best friend are able to sit together, working companionably, there's no harm in letting them. Siblings are often able to sit together around the dining table, working on homework and occasionally helping each other. Of course you shouldn't allow this kind of communal studying if it's slowing anybody down, but working together may actually help.

✎ **Redirect younger siblings.** While siblings who are close in age may be able to sit at the table and do homework together, younger siblings can be a problem. A toddler who longs to grab his older brother's ruler when he's working on a math project needs to be distracted. But your efforts to distract the little one may rouse jealousy in your older child. Jane C. describes what happens at her house: "When Joe sits down to do his homework, I try to take Will off and do something with him so he won't bother Joe. But then Joe feels that Will's having all the fun."

Keeping your younger child occupied while being available to help your older child can pose a real dilemma. One solution is to find a parallel activity your younger child can do. If your younger child is a toddler, try putting him in the high chair for a snack while your older child works. Give your older child a snack to munch on while he works too and everybody may be able to get along peaceably. If your younger child is preschool age, he may be happy if you give him some "homework" of his own. Let him sit nearby and color in his coloring book or do a crafts project.

"**B**obby's a morning person. He's always gotten up at around 6:00. So now he does homework in the morning. I give him his breakfast and then he sits down to work on his homework before he gets dressed."

—JANICE L.

Fourth through Sixth Grades

By the time your child enters fourth grade, homework will probably become more demanding. On the one hand, he should be used to the idea of homework now so he should be more or less resigned to nightly assignments. But the work itself will be more challenging. In particular, he'll probably be called upon to do long-term projects that require organization and planning. All of the suggestions given here for first-through third-graders still apply, along with these new ideas:

✎ **Consider cutting back on after-school activities.** As your child's homework load increases you may find that he simply has too much to do. Today's children are often "overbooked" as never before. If your child has karate lessons on Monday and Wednesday, piano on Tuesday, pottery on Thursday, and French class on Friday, he may not have the time or energy to do his homework. For many families, fourth grade marks a "moment of truth" watershed when parents and children have to decide which after-school activities are most important. Be sure to solicit your child's opinion on this matter rather than deciding on your own that karate is more important than French, for example. If your child hates to give up these activities, you may be able to schedule some for weekends when there is more time.

If both parents are working in the afternoons, it may not be possible for your child to come home and do homework in the afternoon. But it might be possible to investigate a different form of after-school care that provides for study time. Some schools offer after-school study hall. If this isn't available in your community, consider arranging for him to come home to a babysitter a couple of times a week, or ask a neighborhood family day-care provider to supervise homework.

Unfortunately, the increase in your child's homework load may make it difficult for him to have daily playdates or to play with neighborhood children each evening. Since play is a very important part of every child's growth and development, try not to cut back on socialization more than you have to. Maybe you can allow playdates two or three times a week instead of every night and concentrate on homework the other nights. And make sure to provide play opportunities on the weekend.

✎ **Help him get organized.** As a working person, you almost certainly use some system of record keeping to remind yourself of the calls you have to make, your appointments, and your deadlines. When your child begins to have assignments that require long-range planning, he too needs a way of keeping track.

At first, sit down and plan with your child. Later, encourage him to make his own schedule. If he makes a major blunder in planning (deciding to do all his week's work on Thursday night, for example), he's probably not ready to plan autonomously. But let him make a few small mistakes, so he can learn how to plan successfully.

There are a number of different ways of keeping track of assignments. Let your child choose the method that appeals to him. Most methods employ the kinds of intriguing "grown-up" stationery supplies that kids love. Here are some possibilities:

- *An assignment book.* This is a popular approach and it's a good one because an assignment book can travel to and from school with your child. Let your child pick out an attractive spiral notebook. If he uses a binder, have him pick a notebook that can snap into his binder. Show him how to start on a new page in the notebook each week. As the teacher gives each assignment, he should write it down on the left-hand page, along with the date when it's due. Later on, he should use the right-hand page to make up a schedule. If he has to do a book report, for example, he might decide to read the book on Monday and Tuesday, jot down his ideas on Wednesday and write the finished report on Thursday.

- *A calendar.* If your child's teacher hands out written assignments, your child doesn't need an assignment book, but he still needs a way of keeping track. Let him buy a calendar—either an interesting datebook or a great wall calendar. Make sure to get a calendar with big spaces for writing in the assignments. Then he can make a note on each day an assignment is due as well as schedule the days when he should work on his assignments ("study spelling words," "go to the library," etc.). Encourage your child to cross off each assignment (or part of an assignment) as he does it—it's a satisfying feeling to see how much you've accomplished.

- *Post-It Notes.* This is an appealingly gimmicky way of achieving the same goal as with the calendar. Let your child buy some Post-It Notes and write each assignment (or part of an assignment) on a separate note, along with the day it has to be accomplished. Let him stick the Post-It Notes up over his desk (if he uses one) or his homework shelf. Then he can tear off a note, crumple it up, stomp on it a few times, and throw it away, as he accomplishes each task. He may like to use a different color Post-It for each subject or for different days of the week.

- *The teacher's assignment sheet.* Some teachers make organizing easy for children by handing out a Xeroxed sheet for each assignment, sometimes even writing the date the assignment is due on the top of the sheet. Let your child print his own schedule for accomplishing the assignment on the top of the assignment sheet and tape it up over his desk or homework shelf.

- *A homework folder.* Let your child buy a special folder with pockets on each inside flap. (Again, if he keeps a binder, get a folder with three-ring holes that will fit into the binder.) He can write down his assignments on a single sheet of paper and put this, along with any printed assignments from the teacher, on one side of the folder. Finished assignments and works in progress can go on the other side.

Help your child to see these kinds of organizational devices as fun

The Complete Book Bag

Have you looked inside your child's backpack or book bag lately? Pretty horrifying, huh? A recent inspection of my daughter's backpack included, among other items, three plastic bags containing old snacks in various stages of decay, a pair of socks, three dried-out markers, three marker caps, and four out-of-date bus passes.

A child's backpack is his personal property and I think it's best not to be too rigid in demanding that it be kept in pristine condition. However, you should encourage your child to clean his pack out occasionally. Otherwise it will become hard to keep his homework organized.

It's essential that your child have a carrying case that zips shut so that no homework can get lost as it travels to and from school. A backpack is the ideal choice since it's easy to carry, but a zippered gym bag, shoulder bag, or other carrier can also work. When shopping for a backpack or book bag, look for these qualities:

- Lightweight but high-quality construction, with tight stitching and well-padded straps
- Sufficient roominess to accommodate a binder and books comfortably
- Lots of compartments for storing writing utensils, lunch money, baseball cards, and other essentials as well as school books
- An appealing design that your child will be proud to carry to and from school

rather than extra work. Maybe he'd like to use a different-colored marker for each day of the week or for each subject area. Maybe he'd like to put a sticker on his calendar each time he finishes an assignment.

✎ **Eliminate telephone calls.** During the second half of the elementary school years, your child is likely to become an avid telephone conversationalist. You'll probably ask (as your parents so often asked each other), "They see each other all day long—what can they find to talk about?" Your child's homework sessions are likely to drag on forever if he's allowed to come to the phone every time one of his friends calls.

Ron Benson, a teacher in the Williamsville Central School District in New York, conducted a study in which he asked ninety-three sixth-graders to list the five most common disturbances that distract them from doing their homework. Fifty-two percent of the students said that the telephone was the most troublesome homework distraction. "Pupils explained that this distraction occurred when the phone rang or when they talked on it," Benson writes. "Curiosity about who was calling and why often distracted their attention."

When his friends call for your child during his homework time, tell them that he's busy and will call them back at a specified time. Better yet, unplug the phone and let the answering machine take messages.

✎ **When he's ready, wean your child away from the kitchen table.** There's no need to press this point because your child will start using his own room sooner or later. But do suggest to him occasionally that he might be more comfortable in his own private space.

✎ **Provide research books.** As your child's homework becomes more sophisticated, he'll begin to need a small reference library. You may simply want to assemble the family's reference books, or buy special ones for him. In any case, make sure they're close at hand, either near his desk, on his homework shelf, or in a bookcase near the place where he does his work.

Your child should certainly have a dictionary. Choose one that is readable and has large type. You may want to buy a junior dictionary written especially for children (such as the *Macmillan Dictionary for Children*), but a good all-purpose dictionary will do. A thesaurus is a

The Joy of Folders

You know that jumble of papers your kid dumps out of his backpack when he comes home from school each night? Well, it doesn't have to be that way. Really. Take him to a stationery store and let him pick out some supplies that will help him keep his schoolwork organized.

One of the best—and most popular—products on the market is the Trapper Keeper, a large binder that stores individual folders as well as paper.

If binders are "out" at your child's school, let him buy several different-colored folders and ask him to keep papers from each of his subjects in the different folders. If he has certain enrichment activities—music, science, and so on—that he only attends once or twice a week, he may be able to lighten his load by keeping those folders at home. Make sure he writes the name of these special activities on his calendar so that he remembers to bring the folders on the given days. Have him buy a separate folder for school newsletters and other notices that are supposed to come home to you.

good tool for young writers. If you don't know how to use a thesaurus, acquaint yourself with this valuable tool and teach your child how to use it too. An atlas will also come in handy.

Deciding whether to invest in an encyclopedia is a tough call. They are expensive and become outdated; on the other hand, they are invaluable research tools and can save you many trips to the library. Consider buying a single-volume encyclopedia, such as *The New Columbia Encyclopedia*. If you're going to spring for a multivolume set, *The World Book* is a good choice. Make sure your child understands the difference between summarizing information gleaned from an encyclopedia and plagiarizing an encyclopedia entry.

Encourage your child to use these reference tools by using them yourself. If you're not sure how a word is spelled or what it means, let your child see you looking it up in the dictionary. If the family is discussing electricity and you realize you don't actually know what causes lightning, look it up in the encyclopedia.

"As a teacher I often had 'homework' of my own to do in the early evening. I found that by sitting down at the dining room table together with my children, we all got our work done and enjoyed some quiet time together. Indirectly, I suspect I was also presenting a model for getting a task done. My daughter learned at first hand that sometimes I, too, made mistakes and had to start over or that I needed to use a dictionary or take a break. Indeed, we often took a break together. She also knew I was there or nearby and available for questions that came up. *Without doing homework for her,* I was doing it with her and helping to establish long-term work habits that paid off in greater independence when she reached high school."

—JOANNE OPPENHEIM, writing in *The Elementary School Handbook*

Young children—even great big sixth-graders!—need structure. The advice and suggestions in this chapter are designed to help you create a structure in which homework can be accomplished in your house.

It will take time to teach your child to sit down at a certain time of day, to keep track of his homework assignments, to work without interruption, and so on. There will be setbacks, mistakes, and regressions, just as there were when your child was learning to walk, to use the toilet, and to use good table manners when he eats. Just as he needed your help with those developmental stages, so does he now. Just as those activities became second nature to him over time, so will doing homework independently develop over time.

Many common homework problems can be resolved just by following these simple suggestions. Tougher problems will require more creative solutions. For help with "I can't," "I won't," and other tough homework problems, read on.

FOUR

"I Can't!"

et's say you've made a schedule for your child to do her homework and you've agreed on a place where she can work. Her books and supplies are neatly arranged on a homework shelf near her work space and she's sitting down, ready to work. She opens her notebook, looks at her assignment, slumps down in her chair and wails: "I can't do it!" Or, "I don't get it!" Or, "It's too hard!"

What's going on? One of three things is probably happening:

1. Your child has fallen behind the rest of her class in this particular skill area (or maybe in all areas). She hasn't understood the lesson on which the homework is based and therefore can't do the homework, which is designed to drill, review or extend the classwork.

2. The homework is inappropriate for your child's grade level. Neither she nor any of her classmates can possibly complete it without help from their parents. The teacher may in fact expect parents to help, or she may simply have misjudged the class's ability to complete the assignment.

3. Although she's capable of doing the work, your child thinks she's not able to do it alone. It may be that she's intimidated by the process of doing homework and needs you to ease her into it. Or it may be that she is using this as an opportunity to get your attention and help.

Talk to Her Teacher

The first two possibilities involve your child's relationship with the school; the third involves your child's relationship with you. The first thing to do in any of these cases, though, is to schedule a meeting with your child's teacher.

Teachers, like the rest of us, are busy people. Ideally, the teacher will be glad to hear from you and will set aside enough time to discuss your concerns. You can make the most of this time by planning ahead and organizing your thoughts. Use the same skills you would use to prepare for a meeting with a business associate. Here are some suggestions:

✎ **Make an appointment for a conference.** In addition to your one or two formal conferences each school year, you're entitled to schedule special conferences to discuss specific concerns. It's often better to arrange a specific time and date with the teacher than to try to communicate with her while she's dismissing her class at the end of the day.

✎ **State the reason for the conference.** Even the most sympathetic teacher probably won't allot more than half an hour for a conference. Make sure she knows exactly what you want to discuss. For example, at the beginning of the conference, you might say, "Janet has been having trouble doing her math homework by herself. I'm concerned about why she has a problem and what we can do to help her."

✎ **Approach the teacher in a positive way.** Even if you're angry about something you perceive the teacher to be doing, it won't help to come across in an aggrieved, aggressive manner. Try to start out saying something positive, like, "Overall, Janet seems to be having a good year in school. She's enjoyed the reading you've assigned and is getting along well with her peers. But math seems to be a problem . . ." Look at the teacher as your ally, not your adversary, and try to enlist her help in resolving the problem.

✎ **Tell the teacher what you think is going on.** Sometimes children's versions of the facts differ significantly from the teacher's. For example, you might report that "Janet tells me there's no time in class for you to explain the math homework and that's why she doesn't know how to do the homework." The teacher may report that Janet stares out the window during math class.

✎ **Ask the teacher to be candid.** Some teachers are reluctant to distress parents with bad news. But you'll be better equipped to help your child when you have all the facts.

✎ **Collaborate with the teacher to resolve the problem.** Keep an open mind when you talk to your child's teacher and try to map out a strategy together. At the end of the conference, state out loud what it is you've decided together. For example, you might say, "Until Janet catches up with her math, I'll go over her homework with her each night. In the meantime, you'll work with her in class to make sure she understands the assignments."

✎ **Stay in touch.** Let your child's teacher know how you think your mutual strategy is working. If the problem continues, schedule another conference to troubleshoot some more.

Ideally, the first conference you hold with your child's teacher will give you some insight into what is really going on. For example, if the teacher reports that your child is having trouble keeping up with the reading assignments in class, you will understand why she needs help at home. If the teacher says your child has no problem at all reading at school, you need to find out why she's asking for help at home.

Once you've got a handle on what's really going on, you can begin to map a strategy for helping your child.

When Your Child Falls Behind

"The biggest problem with falling behind," says Jackie Kibbe, a third-grade teacher in New York, "is that it's so hard to get back on track.

Every day you go into school and the teacher is giving a lesson that's based on the previous lesson, which you didn't understand. It's crucial that a kid who's fallen behind get back on track as quickly as possible."

Confer with your child's teacher and try to discover why she has fallen behind. Maybe she was out sick and missed an important lesson. Maybe she's been distracted because her team is heading for the play-offs or her grandmother is visiting for the week. Maybe something is bothering her—a fight with a close friend or problems at home, for example. Or it may just be that she didn't understand the information when it was explained and hasn't gotten the help she needs to catch up.

You also need to rule out the possibility of a learning disability or other general condition that may be interfering with her learning. If she's been in school for a few years and has been doing fine up until now, it's unlikely that she has suddenly developed a learning disability. But if this subject area has always been a problem or if she's having a particularly hard time absorbing new material, you may want to have her tested. You'll find more information on learning disabilities on pp. 193–196.

If you're confident that your child's lapse is only temporary, decide with the teacher what can be done to help her. If she has the time, the teacher may be willing to devote extra attention to your child, either before or after school or during the day. She's really the ideal person to help her, since she can tell—from watching her in class and checking her homework assignments—where the problem areas are.

Most teachers, unfortunately, don't have the time to offer their students the kind of individualized attention your child needs. Can *you* help her? You can, if you understand the material yourself and if you and your child are able to work together without initiating World War III. If so, by all means work with your child to help her understand the material. You'll find suggestions in Chapters 6–8 to help you with specific ideas.

Helping your child with homework isn't always easy. As Joanne Oppenheim says, "Helping with homework calls for a delicate kind of balancing act. Knowing how many questions you should answer or when to stop and throw it back to the child really depends on multiple factors. . . . You really need to know both your child and yourself very well. For example, if you are a stickler for grammar and spelling or if you are bubbling over with ideas for a story, you may be the wrong person to read through your child's writing assignment."

If you decide to help your child get back on track, you'll be doing more than just helping her with her homework. You'll be helping her develop the skills she needs to do her homework. For a few minutes each day, you'll actually be her teacher. Try to work with your child on the basic concepts and leave the solving of math problems or the writing of sentences up to her. You don't want her to become dependent on your help.

If you are tutoring your child at home, Jackie Kibbe says, "I suggest you get a different textbook from the one the class is using. That way she doesn't have to feel that she's fallen behind and it won't affect her confidence. You'll just be working together in another textbook."

Kibbe offers another useful tip: "Go back to a point in the text before the problem began. For example, if she's learning to carry numbers, go back to easier arithmetic problems that she can do. That way she'll be reminded that there are math problems she *can* do. She needs that sense of competence and mastery. Then work forward, covering the territory that has created the problem and bringing her up to the level of the rest of the class."

If you don't feel you can teach your child yourself, there may be someone else in your family who can help. Eileen Wrightsman, a sixth-grade teacher in a rural school district, says, "Often when a parent tries to help there's conflict. Sometimes it's better if an older brother or sister—someone who is familiar with the material and whom the child looks up to—helps. In one case recently, one of my students got a big boost from her mother's boyfriend. The girl's mom was working evenings and didn't have a lot of time and the girl was struggling with basic math facts. This person (the boyfriend) just got through to her that there are certain tricks you can use and she was also receiving remedial help at school; it just kind of clicked and that extra bit of attention she got from him really did help."

Staying Back

If your child consistently falls behind the rest of the class and there's no sign that a learning disability or a temporary distraction is at fault, it may be that she's been placed in the wrong grade level. Especially if she is among the youngest in the class, she may just be developmentally unprepared for this grade. You need to consider holding her back a year.

Of course you'll want to approach this decision with care. No matter how delicately worded, the idea of holding a child back has a certain unfortunate (and wrong) connotation of failure. On the other hand, consistently performing below the rest of the class can seriously undermine a child's self-confidence and lead to behavioral problems.

Keeping a child back a year does not mean that she's not as bright or as talented as children her own age who move on. It just means that she's better suited to a less demanding curriculum. She will learn more in a setting where she can handle the materials she's given than she will in a classroom where the work is beyond her.

A good way to help your child accept the idea of staying back a year is to change schools. This way you can explain that the new school is organized differently and in this school she belongs in the third grade while at the old school she would have gone into fourth. Your child won't have to be in a school with former classmates who are now ahead of her. An even better alternative (which unfortunately is not available in many communities) would be to place her in a school with mixed age grouping, where, for instance, she could "repeat" second grade in a mixed second- and third-grade class.

Many children finally hit their stride and begin to blossom intellectually when they change to a grade level that's more appropriate to their skills.

Tutoring

If the teacher is unavailable to help your child and if you feel that you're not the best person to teach her, you may want to consider hiring a tutor. A good tutor can make an enormous difference to a child's education. Many of the parents I've spoken to about homework have told me that their children's tutors "turned him around," "got her over the hump," "gave him the confidence he needed," and otherwise improved their children's performance in class.

A tutor doesn't have to be paid professional. Ask your child's teacher whether there is a peer tutoring program at her school. These innovative programs match students with children their own age or slightly older who help them grasp the concepts they need.

If you decide to hire a tutor, ask your child's teacher for recommendations. You might also ask other parents and check ads in the local newspaper. Regardless of who recommends the tutor, you should also ask him or her for references. Call other parents who have worked with the tutor and ask them how long the tutor worked with the child, how the child liked him or her, how much the tutoring helped, and so on.

The rates for tutoring vary greatly from community to community. Tutoring can be costly, but it's far less expensive than sending your child to a private school. Tutoring may prove to be a good way to fill in the gaps in your child's public school education.

Arrange for your child to meet the prospective tutor once before signing up for a series of sessions. Try to match your child up with someone whom she likes and feels comfortable with. Once the tutor has met with the child and looked over her work, talk with the tutor and your child about the goals of the tutoring and establish a basic time frame in which you hope to accomplish those goals.

When you hire a tutor, make sure your child's teacher knows what's going on. Try to arrange for the teacher and the tutor to talk so that they can coordinate their efforts to help your child.

In the last decade, a number of tutoring centers have sprung up around the country. Modeled on the SAT preparation centers that have been doing good business for years, these tutoring centers offer training to students from elementary years on up. Tutoring centers have all the pros and cons of any institutionalized setting. Because each center has a curriculum for every subject area, there tends to be less truly individualized attention than your child would receive with her own tutor. But some centers offer imaginative, "fun" programs that kids actually enjoy. Overall, tutoring centers can be as good or bad as individual tutors. You need to check out the center carefully and solicit references just as you would with an individual tutor.

The point of tutoring is to help your child understand basic concepts that she somehow missed in class. In many cases tutoring lasts for a finite period of time, until your child is working at the same level as her classmates. Sometimes if one particular subject is an ongoing problem, or your child has a learning disability in this area, then tutoring may last longer.

Try to avoid, however, hiring someone who bills himself as a "homework tutor." Homework tutors sit with children while they do their homework and help them with every phase of the operation. Rather than working with your child for a finite period, the homework tutor could become a regular fixture in your home. Since your goal is to see that your child learns to do her own homework independently, hiring someone to hover over her while she does it is rarely a good idea. It may be helpful for your child to sit with someone for a few afternoons and get some pointers on organizing and executing her homework efficiently, but a homework tutor should not be a part of her daily routine.

When the Homework Is Inappropriate

Teachers use homework as an index to determine how well their students are absorbing the lessons they hear in class. If the majority of the class is turning in correct homework, the teacher knows that she is teaching to the students' skill level. If the students have trouble completing a particular assignment, the teacher knows she needs to go over the material on which the assignment was based.

Sometimes when a student complains that she can't do an assignment, parents intervene and walk the child through the homework.

How to Hire a Tutor

Here are some of the questions you should ask a prospective tutor:

✎ **"What are your credentials?"** Is the tutor a certified teacher? Is she working as a teacher now? What other related experience does she have?

✎ **"What age level do you usually work with?"** A first-grade teacher may not be the best person to work with your sixth-grader.

✎ **"How much do you charge?"** Will you be charged if your child cancels a session?

✎ **"How often will you want to meet with my child?"** Once a week is common but your child may need more attention.

✎ **"Where do you do your tutoring?"** It may be more convenient for you if the tutor comes to your home. On the other hand, your child may concentrate more if she travels to the tutor's home (or to a tutoring center).

✎ **"Do you have a special approach?"** A good tutor will have a strategy for teaching your child. Find out what she has in mind.

If enough parents do this, the majority of the homework will come back correct and the teacher will assume that she is giving appropriate homework and will give more of the same. It's a vicious cycle.

To break the cycle, you need to speak up. If you feel that your child's teacher is giving inappropriate homework, talk to a few of her classmates' parents. If they tell you that their children are able to do the homework independently, in a reasonable amount of time, then it's possible that your child is the only one—or one of the few—who is having trouble in this skill area. But if other parents tell you that their children, too, are having trouble, it's probably the teacher's assignments that are at fault.

You'll be doing the teacher a favor if you make an appointment to see her and tell her that your child is having trouble completing the homework independently. Use the same positive negotiation strategies described on pp. 62–63. Urge the other parents with whom you've spoken to do the same thing. Or you might ask the class PTA representative to intervene on your behalf.

Teachers are often grateful to receive this kind of feedback. "I'd just assumed that the class had understood our unit on electricity because the homework I gave was coming back complete," one young teacher told me. "Then a few parents spoke up and said they'd had to help their kids with the assignment and later I realized that no one had really understood. I was surprised more parents didn't come to me."

Occasionally you'll run across a teacher who won't change, even in the face of evidence that's she's giving too difficult assignments. In that case, you'll have to decide for yourself how you can support your child through a difficult year.

"Last year was terrible. Elizabeth would come home on Monday with long lists of assignments. There was at least an hour of homework a night and in the beginning, when we were still getting the hang of it, it sometimes took two hours. The class was a combined first, second, and third grade and even though Elizabeth was only in second grade, she felt badly if she couldn't do as much as the third-graders. The teachers wanted the parents to help, to check the homework and do a lot of it with them—for example, the science projects.

"At the conference the teachers said she should only be doing forty-five minutes of homework. But when I would tell her to stop after forty-five minutes, she'd insist on going on. She didn't want to get in trouble.

"Eventually, she learned to do the homework and she became very responsible about it. Under the circumstances, I think she did very well and she earned praise from her teachers, but she didn't feel very smart. And she had so much work to do that she stopped reading for pleasure altogether.

"This year she's in a different school and there's very little homework. I feel it's a much-deserved vacation."

—ELLEN Z.

Dear Ms. Jones

If your child is legitimately unable to complete a particular assignment because she didn't understand the material covered in class, you can ask her to do as much of the assignment as she can, and then write a note to the teacher, something like this:

Dear Ms. Jones:
Sandy wasn't able to complete tonight's homework be-cause she doesn't understand what homonyms are. Could you please help her with this concept?

Sincerely,
Eleanor Smith

On the rare occasion when you want to excuse your child from homework for a night—when, for example, she's not feeling well or her sister's performing in her class play—you should certainly write to her teacher and explain the situation. If you can let the teacher know in advance that your child won't be able to do her homework, by all means do.

When "I Can't" Is an Emotional Plea

Okay. You've ruled out the possibility that your child's homework is actually too hard for her. You've determined that the assignment itself is appropriate for someone of your child's grade level and abilities. So why is she still whining and complaining and insisting that she can't do her homework by herself?

Let me guess. Your evening goes something like this. When you tell her it's time to do her homework, your child sits down fairly willingly and opens her books. After a quick glance at her assignment she complains, "I don't get it!" You come over and look at the assign-ment and try to explain it to her. She nods, looks down at the page and demands, as you sidle away from the table, "Sit with me!" With a longing look at the dishes you're trying to get done before bedtime, you sit down "just for a minute," while your child gets under way.

You help her through the first problem and then get back to the dishes. You've scrubbed one pot when your child bursts into tears, throws her books to the floor and shouts angrily, "I need you to sit with me! Don't go away!" Whereupon you shout back, "That's enough of that, young lady!" And so on . . .

If you stop and think about it, the scenario I've just described (or whatever comparable scenario goes on at your house) doesn't really have a lot to do with education. It does, however, have everything to do with relationships and with discipline. As you know from other aspects of your parenting experience, the key to effective discipline is setting reasonable limits and sticking to them.

Some books and magazine articles about homework tell parents exactly what limits they ought to set. In most cases, the writers of these books and articles tell parents that homework is the exclusive property of students; they—the parents—should provide a time and a place and insist that the students complete their work independently. I think that advice is unrealistic.

The limits you set will depend on many factors—your child's age, her temperament, how comfortable your child is with the material she's learning, how good the school is, how much attention the teacher is able to give her, and what kind of relationship you have with your child.

Up to now, you may not have thought about homework as a disciplinary issue. You may be handling each evening's homework as a new experience, sometimes sitting with your child and going through the assignment together, at other times refusing to listen to her complaints and so on. Now though, take some time to think about how you want to handle homework. Figure out what limits you want to set and vow to keep them.

As I've said, setting limits is a wholly personal matter. Here are some guidelines, however, that may help you to think about the limits that will be appropriate for your child:

✎ **Kindergarten and first grade.** A very young child's unwillingness to do her homework alone can be a form of separation anxiety. Staying nearby now won't make her utterly dependent on you in the future. Remember how she used to need you to come along when she went to other kids' houses to play? She probably can't wait to say goodbye when you drop her off now. By the same token, she may need you to be nearby when she embarks on this new, so grown-up project. Insisting that she go off and do her homework by herself may just backfire on you, as it will make her more anxious and dependent. As she works, praise her efforts and draw attention to how well she's handling the work. "Wow—you did that whole assignment," you might say, or, "Great, you answered every question."

✎ **Second and third grades.** By the time she starts second grade, your child will probably have had enough experience of homework to be ready to let go of you and do much of it on her own. A good strategy at this age is to be nearby without actually sitting with your child. If you're busily engaged, perhaps making dinner or doing your own work that you've brought home from the office, your child will feel less lonely without being as dependent on your presence. When she asks for help, you might have her read the directions aloud to you and then tell you what she thinks they mean. Once you're sure she understands the assignment, tell her you expect her to complete it on her own. It will help if you establish a reward system that inspires her to work on her own. "You do this assignment by yourself," you might say, "and then I'll play a game with you." (Or read a book or take a walk.) That way your child is assured of your attention in a positive context and won't be as inclined to attract the negative attention of arguing with you about whether she can do her homework.

✎ **Fourth through sixth grades.** Once your child is in the fourth grade, separation anxiety is probably no longer an issue. She may, however, continue to use homework as a way of attracting your attention, even if it's negative attention. By this time, you can be comfortable being very clear in your expectation that she will do her homework herself. At this age it may be helpful for your child to move out of the kitchen or dining room and into her own room so that she's not distracted by what you're doing. Tell her you're available if she has problems but you can't go over her assignment one step at a time. If she's doing a sheet of math questions, for example, she could skip the ones that are difficult and save up her questions for you. If you're sure she can do the work by herself, be firm in insisting she handle it on her own. Offer a motivation that's appropriate to her age: if she finishes her homework and does a good job, she can ride her bike until dark, for example.

Homework and Gender: "Girls Aren't Good at Math!"

Rob and Mira Z. are feminist parents who have done their best to ensure that their daughters Sarah and Joanne are being raised in a nonsexist environment. The other day, Joanne, who's in sixth grade, was struggling over her math assignment. When Mira urged her to keep trying, Joanne complained, "Oh, Mom—I'm just not any good at math. You know girls aren't good at math!"

Despite all of Rob and Mira's efforts, Joanne had somehow internalized a negative image of her abilities as a female. And she was using that image as an excuse to try to avoid doing her math homework.

The perception that girls aren't good at math—or science or computer technology—can be extremely damaging to girls. It means that many adults—including teachers and parents—expect less of girls in these areas. It's a built-in excuse for girls to fail and can become a self-fulfilling prophecy.

Interestingly, girls perform as well as or better than boys in math in the early elementary grades. But sometime during adolescence, most girls lose their math momentum, and boys begin to outperform them. By the time girls leave high school, most lag well behind boys in math skills, scientific knowledge, and computer expertise.

In case the seriousness of this condition hasn't struck you, consider a 1976 study conducted at the University of California at Berkeley. Sociologist Lucy Sells found that 92% of entering female freshmen had taken so little math in high school that they were only qualified for five majors: elementary education, guidance and counseling, humanities, music, and social sciences.

Researchers have postulated a number of explanations for girls' declining interest in math. Some argue that mathematical ability is sex-linked, so that boys naturally achieve more than girls. Others argue that boys receive more attention and encouragement in the classroom as well as more pressure to succeed from their parents. Another theory is that adolescent girls themselves perceive math to be unfeminine and seek to dissociate themselves from it.

" I have a little math phobia myself but I'd like my daughter not to be afraid of math. I'm very conscious of presenting math in a positive way. We play math games around the dinner table. Or we'll write out math problems for each other—I write one for her to do and then she writes one out for me. Although she's only in second grade, she has figured out what multiplication is and we do drills together—because she likes to, not because I sit down and make her. Or I'll say, 'I need seventy-five cents. Can you get it out of my purse for me?' "

—ANN P.

If there are biological factors predisposing boys to outperform girls in math and science, there is little we can do to change this condition. But we owe it to our daughters to work hard to change their environment so that they aren't led to turn away from math and science. Here are some tacks you can take:

✎ **Expect your daughter to do well in math and science.** Praise and compliment her on her math and science work. Mira's response to Joanne's complaint that "girls aren't good at math" was twofold. First, she explained that girls can do just as well at math as boys can. And second, she commented on how well Joanne had done in the past. She said that even though Joanne was tackling a tough assignment, she, Mira, was sure she could handle it.

✎ **Tell your daughter why math and science are important.** Talk about the career opportunities that are open to women who pursue math and science. Point out the many ways you use math and science in your everyday adult life—from balancing the checkbook to fertilizing and reseeding your lawn.

✎ **Don't give her an excuse to fail.** If you did poorly in math or science yourself, you may tend to make light of your daughter's efforts. A comment like "Oh, she's just like me—I can't add either!" will ultimately be undermining.

✎ **Provide math-related games and exercises.** The skill-building techniques and games mentioned throughout Part II are certainly as important for girls as for boys. Your daughter may not naturally gravitate toward a game like Uno, but try it out: she may love it!

✎ **Provide games that build science and computer skills.** Many traditionally "boys'" games, like construction sets and model kits, foster science skills by teaching boys how to take things apart and put them back together again. Make sure your daughter has these kinds of toys too. If you have a home computer, let your daughter play computer games as well as use educational programs. The more comfortable she feels around a computer keyboard, the better.

✎ **Make math a part of life.** For many of us, it's easy to make books and reading an everyday part of life. You may have to work a little harder to show your daughter how math fits in, but make the effort. How many windows are there in the apartment building across the street? If we multiply the number of windows across by the number of floors, we'll get the answer. How many daffodil bulbs do we need to buy to plant in our front garden? Let's measure the garden and find out.

Gender discrimination in the classroom is another matter of concern to caring parents. Myra Sadker, an education professor at American University, has done research in the ways teachers respond to boys and girls in the classroom. She finds that boys are eight times more likely to call out in class than girls. Furthermore, while teachers are relatively tolerant of boys calling out, they tend to reprimand girls who do the same thing. When a girl comes to a teacher for help, the teacher is likely to do the work for her while when a boy comes to the teacher for help, she is more likely to show him how to complete the assignment.

If you have the opportunity to spend a day in your child's classroom, watch out for this tendency to give boys preferential treatment. If you find your child's teacher fostering an environment in which boys are freer to speak than girls, point out your observations to her. Chances are, her actions are unconscious. If you make your remarks in a spirit of collaboration, your child's teacher may try to change. In the meantime, make sure your daughter gets lots of encouragement when she speaks up at home.

. . .

The kid who says, "I can't do my homework" is asking you directly for help. Whether you help her by sitting down and showing her how to do her math problems or by hiring a tutor or by setting and enforcing clearer limits, you'll be meeting her conscious yearning for parental intervention. Read on for ways of working with a child who expresses her need for help less directly.

Help for *You*

The National Committee for Citizens in Education is an advocate for citizens who want to improve their children's education. You can call the organization's toll-free helpline for help with questions about homework as well as other educational issues.

1-800-NETWORK (638-9675)

FIVE

"I Won't!"

I t's rare for an elementary school student to flat-out refuse to do his homework. Most children under twelve still feel that they "ought" to follow the rules their parents and teachers have laid down for them. Although an adolescent may reach a stage where he consciously rebels against homework, an elementary school student usually believes he should do his homework even though he doesn't want to.

But elementary school students express their reluctance to do homework just the same. They use a variety of excuses that amount to a campaign of passive resistance. Do any of these phrases sound familiar?

✎ **"Not now, later."** This is probably the most popular phrase among homework resisters. Kids who say they'll do their homework after dinner or in a little while or when they finish watching TV genuinely expect to do their homework sooner or later but their strong desire not to do it at all makes them want to put it off as long as possible. Of course if they wait long enough to get around to doing their homework, they'll probably be tired and irritable—not the best

state of mental preparation—and may manage to get out of it altogether.

✎ **"I don't have any homework."** Claiming not to have any homework is another popular dodge. The kid who says he doesn't have
homework may not be telling an out-and-out lie so much as expressing
a wish. Maybe there was some homework but he got a little done on
the bus and can probably finish it up before school tomorrow. . . .
This kind of avoidance is a serious matter but it needs to be handled
with compassion.

✎ **"I left my book at school."** Once is an accident, twice is careless, three times is probably homework avoidance. You don't need an
advanced degree in psychology to figure out that the kid who consistently leaves his homework at school has devised a strategy (probably
unconscious) for avoiding doing it.

These kinds of avoidance techniques are just about guaranteed to
get parents hot under the collar. While we'd like to handle our children rationally and calmly, homework often brings out the worst in
us. I'm willing to bet that if Mother Teresa ever had any children of
her own, folks would have heard her saying, "What do you mean you
left your math book at school *again?*" and "I'm sick and tired of telling
you. I want you to sit down and do your homework and do it now,"
and "You'll never get into a good college if you don't do your homework now."

By now, you and your child may be engaged in a power struggle
over homework. Every exchange you have on the subject may be filled
with anger, accusation and confrontation. It may seem impossible
even to bring the subject up without detonating another depth
charge. Disengaging yourselves from this kind of struggle can be hard,
but rest assured it can be done.

I wish I could offer you a sure-fire remedy that would cure your
child of the "I won'ts." But I don't know your child or your family or
his teacher or his school. As you read the following suggestions, think
about which would work best with your child. You know your child
better than anyone and you are the best judge of how to help him.

Try a Little Empathy

Researchers at the University of Illinois and Loyola University recently did a study designed to track children's emotions. They gave beepers to 480 fifth- through ninth-grade students and asked them to make a record of what they were doing and how they felt every time the beeper went off (about every two hours). Of all their activities, the one the students disliked most was homework. (The one they liked best was sports.)

How would you like to have to do homework? Suppose that on top of everything else you have to get done in the evening, you had to fill in a series of worksheets, write a short essay, and work on a special project? It might be kind of fun at first but I bet the novelty would wear off as you had to do the homework night after night.

You may protest that you do in fact bring work home every night. But at least that is work relating to your chosen profession that you feel a personal commitment to. From your child's perspective, homework may seem arbitrary and irrelevant. And besides, don't you wish you *didn't* have to bring work home? If you had a secretary who could do it for you, wouldn't you gladly hand a lot of it over to him or her?

I'm not saying that all homework is a drag. Homework can be as interesting or as dull as the teacher who assigns it. But some of it is bound to be at least a little dull for your child and it doesn't hurt for you to understand and sympathize.

Ann Rothschild, a philosopher as well as the mother of two elementary school students, describes how she uses empathy to avoid fights with her children over homework: "This week, Will was given a complicated assignment on Monday that was due on Friday. The time pressure made *me* frantic. And when I'm frantic, it ruins our household tranquility. One thing that helps me is to identify with our children instead of the school. I got started this morning and asked him what he had in mind. We started thinking about it and that part was fun. Oliver (my older son) was contributing ideas." Instead of focusing on her own anxiety, Rothschild tried to help her son make his vision of the assignment a reality.

The opposite of empathizing with your child is criticizing him. "Your backpack is a mess—no wonder you lost your assignment." "If you spent less time trading stickers and more time listening to the teacher, you'd understand this assignment." "This paper is so sloppy I can't even read it!" These statements may each be true in their way, but they're guaranteed to undermine a child's self-confidence and make him more belligerent and uncooperative than ever.

You've probably read in other books about the "active listening" approach to child rearing. The idea is that instead of denying or belittling the things our children say to us, we should allow and accept them.

For example, let's say your child tries to avoid doing his homework by saying, "It's too hard. I can't do it. And besides, I'm too tired. I'll do it in the morning." The opposite of active listening would be to answer something like this: "It's not hard at all. You've been doing the same work in class. And what do you mean you're too tired? You weren't tired five minutes ago when you were riding your bike all over the neighborhood." When a parent responds this way, the child feels angry and misunderstood.

The actively listening parent would "mirror" the child's emotions by saying something like: "You're worried that you won't be able to do the work. And you're feeling kind of wiped out after all that bike riding." Feeling that he has your sympathy and compassion, the child is much more likely to knuckle down to the task at hand.

For more information on active listening, you may want to read Nancy Samalin's excellent book, *Loving Your Child Is Not Enough: Positive Discipline That Works* (Penguin). Try using some of these techniques when you're talking to your child about homework. You'll be surprised at how quickly they can defuse a tense situation.

A technique like active listening can be a powerful tool when you're trying to get out of a power struggle with your child. Try to be genuinely compassionate. Don't be afraid to put yourself in your child's shoes. Seeing things from his point of view won't undermine your authority. It will just give you a way of being on his side, where he needs you to be.

"Reading is so important to Frank and me, we really wanted Allison to learn to read. And we were constantly talking about reading and trying to get her to read aloud to us. The result was that she was totally uninterested. She was way behind her class in reading. We made a conscious effort to ease up on the pressure. Whether it was that or just that she was developmentally ready to start reading, she really took off in the third grade."

—SONIA P.

Avoid Pressuring Your Child

While you're looking at things from your child's point of view, take a hard look at your own expectations. Is it possible that you've been putting too much pressure on your child to measure up to your standards? Have you made it clear, subtly or overtly, that you did well in school and you expect your child to as well? (Or worse, that his older brother did well and it's up to him to carry on the family tradition?)

Trying to live up to parental expectations can be very hard on a child. Children react differently to the excessive demands their parents put on them. Some work hard to achieve and receive praise and approval—but often at the cost of spontaneity and enjoyment. Others rebel quietly by avoiding the competition.

Ann Rothschild comments: "We've had major, major fights about homework and piano practice but they're all tied up with my expectations. I find that a helpful approach is to realize that it doesn't have to be perfect. Will is who he is and if his work isn't perfect, who cares? I don't. When I think it through, I realize it's not going to affect his learning. The more I let go, the better it gets."

Beth Teitelman, Associate Director of the Parenting Center at New York's 92nd Street Y, comments, "I find myself yelling at my child about homework and underneath that is my anxiety that she will be a terrible student all her life. But yelling is counterproductive. How she does now is not really a predictor of how she'll do in the future."

Expecting your child to do his homework promptly and conscientiously is not pressuring him. Expecting him to hand in perfect, pristinely neat, and error-free assignments *is* expecting too much. Try easing up on your child and you may be surprised at how quickly he responds.

Teitelman points out that it takes time for children to grow into doing homework responsibly. "It's like so many other issues with children," she says. "Like when will she sleep through the night and when will he tie his own shoes and when will he learn to throw his dirty laundry in the hamper. There's a developmental momentum with these things and kids have to grow into doing homework."

Do you feel that your child has failed if he gets anything less than an A – on his report card? If so, you may have exaggerated expectations. Instead of expressing your dissatisfaction, focus on the ways your child *is* achieving. Teitelman urges, "Never miss an opportunity for pointing out what a good job they've done."

Stick to Your Limits

Your child won't get away with doing his homework at the last minute if you expect him to do it every evening before dinner. Setting and sticking to reasonable limits—the kinds discussed in Chapters 3 and 4—doesn't make you an ogre. Sure, your kid will try to get out of doing homework when you ask him to, but it's your job to be clear and firm. Ultimately, it's a lot easier and healthier for him to know exactly what you expect and that you mean what you say than it is for him to spend every night quarreling with you.

Some parents find it hard to stick to the limits they set. If you have a hard time enforcing other limits too—bedtime, chores, and so on—you may want to give some thought to why this is a problem in your household. Are you afraid of losing your child's affection by telling him he can't do exactly what he wants? For general suggestions on discipline, you may want to read Nancy Samalin's book (mentioned earlier) and also *Who's in Control?* by Dr. Lawrence Balter (Poseidon Press).

Using the suggestions in Chapter 3 as points of departure, devise a homework schedule. Explain your expectations to your child and make it clear that while you are available for certain kinds of help, you cannot accept rude behavior.

Beth Teitelman urges, "Never discuss homework problems during homework time. Wait for a neutral time, like Saturday morning, and then broach the subject with your child. You might introduce the conversation by saying, 'I was reading a book about homework and I was thinking about the way we do homework in our family.' Explain to your child that homework is important and that you need to work together to make sure it is done each night."

"At the beginning of the year, Dana (who's in second grade) really didn't like doing her homework and it took some pushing. I said to her, 'This is something you have to do. I can't sit down and do it for you.' I had to get tough with her. She would cry and whine for a couple of minutes and then she got down to business. Now she doesn't give me any trouble about it."

—CAROL B.

Try Letting Your Child Face the Consequences

What would happen if your child didn't hand in his homework on time? Or if he answered only half the questions on his worksheet? Or if he didn't learn this week's spelling assignment?

In any of these circumstances, your child would have to face the consequences of his actions. And while he may be willing to face your disapproval, threats, and demands, he may be far less willing to risk his teacher's disapproval.

Especially when conflicts over homework have escalated into an ego battle between parent and child it can be very helpful for the parent simply to remove herself from the situation. Essentially, a homework assignment is a contract between your child and his teacher. If he doesn't complete the assignment as required, his teacher will be displeased with him and he will receive a low mark on his work. That may be all the inspiration he needs to start handling homework more responsibly.

Ellen Galinsky, an educator and author of *The Six Stages of Par-*

enthood (Addison-Wesley), says, "One of the reasons I never had trouble with my own children's homework is that I always made it clear that it was their homework and not mine. I was deeply interested, I liked talking to them about it, I always read their papers, I gave them pretests when they needed them and I often read the books they were reading so we could talk about them. But I made it clear that it was not my problem if they didn't do their homework. I didn't spend a lot of time bugging them to do homework.

"With each child, we figured out a schedule for doing homework that matched the child's style—whether it was to do homework right after school or to have a break first, for instance. But if they didn't do their homework it was their problem."

Psychologist Lawrence Balter agrees with Ellen Galinsky about the value of letting children face the consequences of their actions. He adds that this is important to do while they're still in elementary school. "Later on, when their grades matter more, it will be harder for you to do this," he predicts. "It's best that both parent and child get into the habit while the child is young."

Obviously, if your child is genuinely unable to do the work and is having an academic problem or if the teacher expects you to help him with his homework, you can't reasonably take this "sink or swim" attitude. But if the homework monster in your house is essentially a discipline problem, making your child answerable to the teacher instead of you may be quite successful.

"I always ask Amy on Friday evening to tell me what homework she has for the weekend and we set aside time for her to do it. But one Sunday night a few weeks ago, she suddenly remembered that she had a book report due the next day. She stayed up until ten that night to do it and she went to school on Monday with dark circles under her eyes.

"Then, a couple of weeks later, the same thing happened again. Again we let her stay up late to finish her assignment but we warned her that we didn't want this to happen again.

"Push came to shove last Sunday night, when Amy remembered that she had to memorize a list of French vocabulary words for a test. I put my foot down and said I was sorry but bedtime is 8:30 at our house and she'd just have to face the test without having memorized those words. She cried and carried on but we stood firm.

"At school the next day, she had to face the consequences of forgetting her homework assignment. We weren't there to cover for her and she had to accept a poorer mark on her test than she wanted. She was unhappy about it but I don't think she'll forget her weekend homework assignment again soon."

—JOANNE B.

The Cardinal Rule: Never Do Your Child's Homework

When your child is very stubborn, it can be tempting to take the path of least resistance by walking him through his assignment. Ultimately, however, you'll be doing more harm than good. Bear in mind one cardinal rule: you can help your child understand his homework, you can sit with him while he does it, but you should *never do his homework for him.*

Nancy Samalin comments, "As parents we want to be in control of our children. One way to exercise control is to do as much as possible for them. But the more we do for them, the less they do for themselves and the more they depend on us to make decisions for them. We want to make sure they are healthy and strong, so we decide what they will eat. We want them to look attractive, so we select their clothes and tell them what shirt to wear with which pants. We want them to earn A's, so we correct their homework."

Parents doing homework for children is all too common a phenomenon. Writing in *Texas Monthly,* in an article called "Hey Mom, Have I Got an Assignment for You," Prudence Mackintosh confesses her own history of helping her kids with their homework: "Like many parents (mainly mothers) in my Dallas neighborhood, I have been through what we once called junior high three times, once for myself and again for each of my two older sons. I have no advanced degrees for the extra years of classwork, but I do have a measure of expertise in the Mayan civilization, the Ku Klux Klan, and algebraic trains that pass in the night while traveling in opposite directions at varying speeds. My magnum opus, however, is a seventh-grade Alamo diary written on paper that I soaked in tea and coffee grounds, dried in the oven, burned around the edges, and finally stained with the blood of my own finger."

As Prudence Mackintosh ruefully admits later in her article, doing her children's homework was not the best way she could help her children learn and grow. She believes that she and other parents like her can easily become overly identified with their children's work. "The bottom line in success-oriented neighborhoods like mine," she writes, "is that failure isn't permitted."

The thing to remember when you're tempted to do your child's homework for him is that your child *owns* his own homework. When he hands in an essay, that essay should be a reflection of his knowledge and his ability to practice good study habits. It's not a reflection of *your* knowledge or your ability to produce a first-rate piece of writing.

If your child does his own work and hands it in to the teacher, he'll know that if he earns a good mark he earned it all by himself. If he knows that you really deserve much of the credit (and kids are pretty canny about this sort of thing), then he'll know in his heart that he didn't completely "deserve" that good mark.

By the same token, if the homework gets a lower mark than he'd like, your child needs to feel that he is personally responsible for that mark too. If he can secretly pass the blame along to the parent who helped him do the homework, then he won't have to be accountable for the results of his work. Instead of vowing to work harder next time, he'll probably vow to get *you* to work harder!

Mary Jane Saffran, who teaches third-grade students in New York City, comments, "You know when the parents are doing the kids' homework. For instance, I gave my class an assignment to think about the problems in New York City and write down some ideas for improvements that could be made. One kid handed in an essay that began something like, 'First of all, I would look at the socio-economic problems that exist in New York today and then I would utilize all available resources. . . .' Come on—this is a kid whose parents did his assignment for him. It happens a lot."

Doing your child's homework for him undermines the whole purpose of homework. Your child won't be practicing skills he's learned or preparing for the next day's lesson. And the teacher won't have an opportunity to find out how well he's absorbing the information he's been taught. Instead of helping him with any problem areas, the teacher will be trying to build on skills your child hasn't really acquired.

"It's true, I was giving John more help with his homework than he probably needed and somewhere in my mind, I was dimly aware of the fact. But it was still really embarrassing to get a note from his teacher that said, 'Nice work, Mrs. S. Now let's see what John can do.' "

—GLORIA S.

Motivate, Motivate

If you can somehow make your child *want* to do homework, the homework monster will be forced to draw in his claws and sit quietly in the corner. So consider putting together a package of positive reinforcement that makes homework hard to resist. Here are some simple motivational strategies:

✎ **Make it worth his while.** Try using what family therapist Helen Crohn calls "leverage." That's bribes to the rest of us but, as Crohn points out, the word "bribe" has a negative connotation it doesn't always deserve. Is there a movie your child is dying to see? Maybe he can go this weekend if he does all his weekly homework. Does he like to go down the block for dessert? If there's time, maybe he can go after he finishes his homework.

Try to use positive leverage only. That is, don't take away a promised privilege or treat as a punishment for not doing homework. But offer something special if your child dutifully lives up to the limits you've described.

✎ **Make a star chart.** A more formal approach is to use a chart of the sort behavior modification therapists often prescribe. In this case, you might set up a large chart, with the days of the week (or month) written across the top. Down the side you can list some homework tasks, like "brought all my homework home from school," "completed my homework in the time allotted," "turned my homework in on time," and so on.

For each task your child performs, place a gold star, a sticker, or simply a check mark in the appropriate box. As soon as he acquires enough stars (or stickers or checks), you can allow him to trade them in for a particular treat. Again, the trick is to emphasize the positive. Don't punish him for failing to earn all his stars—but wait until he's amassed a specific number of successes before rewarding him.

✎ **Praise and praise again.** Take every opportunity to praise your child. If he manages to bring all his homework home, even if he's unwilling to do it, praise him for that. If he does half his assignment, tell him how well he did that half. The good feelings your praise gives him will make him want to earn more of it. Remember, an ounce of praise is more effective than a pound of criticism.

✎ **Brag about your child.** Another way to praise your child is to let him hear you "showing off" about him. When you're on the phone with Aunt Betty, tell her, "Sam's such a good reader! We can't get to the library often enough to keep him stocked!" You don't have to tell Aunt Betty just now that Sam refuses to do his math homework. Be sure to tell your child, too, when someone else praises him. Tell him, "Your teacher was telling me all about that essay you wrote. She really thought it was terrific."

✎ **Solicit your child's ideas.** Ask your child what would help him to feel better about doing his homework. Would he like to have a snack while he works sometimes? Would a little soft background music be nice? Would he like you to send his little brother next door so that just you and he are in the house together? Help him to feel good about the time he spends doing homework.

When Nothing Seems to Help

As you know from other aspects of your parenting experiences, changes take time. If you make a rule that homework has to be done before dinner every night, you can expect some resistance at first as you enforce this rule. Your child may only begin responding consistently to a behavior chart after he gets his first reward. So give the strategies in this chapter—and throughout the first part of this book —time to take effect.

But if all your efforts seem to fail and you feel like you're running into a brick wall over and over again, it may be time to consider professional help. You might request that your child see the school psychologist for a few sessions, or you might all agree to meet with a family therapist to talk over the problems you're having with homework.

PART TWO

SIX

Empower Your Child

Now that you've taken the time to think about what kinds of problems your child is having with homework, you can begin to make things better. Whether you see your proper role as your child's supervisor or her teacher, her cheering section or her mentor, your task is to help her feel confident about doing her homework.

The key to taming the homework monster is empowering your child. The more capable and self-directed she becomes, the less she'll yell, scream, whine, and complain to you. The strategies in these next chapters will give you the power to help your child do her homework effectively, successfully, and independently.

Chapters 7, 8, and 9 describe what your child is learning in school at every grade level. This part of the book is divided into subject areas —language arts, math, social studies, and science. It tells you what kinds of homework you can expect in each subject and gives you strategies for helping your child do her homework.

Throughout these next few chapters, you will find suggestions that will help your child accomplish her homework tasks and tips to help her improve her skills. Doing these extra activities shouldn't feel burdensome to your child—they're designed to be fun and to feel effortless. But they will directly affect her ability to complete her homework successfully. The more proficient your child becomes the more smoothly both her classwork and her homework will go.

Every school system is different, so that the material your child studies in third grade may be quite different from the material my daughter will study next fall. You may have to skip around in the next few chapters to find the section that applies to your child. For example, many children begin bringing home spelling words to memorize in first grade, so I've included spelling in the chapter on first grade. If your child doesn't bring home spelling words until second grade, you'll have to go back to the earlier chapter.

A Word about Computers

Should you or shouldn't you buy your child a computer?

There's no question that computers are here to stay and that their uses and applications will only increase in the decade to come. If you work with a computer or use one in your home, you already know what a valuable tool it is.

Computers are entering the classroom too, in a flood in some schools and in a trickle in others. The better funded a school system is, the more computers you'll find. When computers were first introduced to the classroom, the emphasis was on teaching children to learn programming and other technical skills. Increasingly, though, educators are finding that computers can be a useful medium for imparting traditional skills, like reading, writing, and math.

During the elementary school years, a home computer is certainly not a necessity. Your child can learn everything she needs to know without a computer. If the school offers computer instruction, your child should be able to learn everything that's being presented right in her classroom.

On the other hand, if you can afford a computer and are willing to take the time to teach your child how to use it, a computer can be a worthwhile investment. In the first place, since your child is almost certain to use a computer at some point in her later educational and professional careers, you'll be giving her a leg up on gaining the proficiency she'll need. And when you introduce the right software, you can help your child learn the skills she needs to do a better job on her homework.

You'll find the names of various software programs listed in each of these next chapters. Addresses and phone numbers of the manufacturers may be found in the Appendix. For names of other software programs, you may want to consult an excellent book, *The Parent's Guide to Educational Software*, by Marion Blank and Laura Berlin (Microsoft Press).

Whatever you do, don't let the computer become a new battleground for homework wars. If you buy a computer, try to help your child have fun with it. The beauty of the software programs recommended in the next few chapters is that they make kids *want* to turn on the computer and "play." Since the computer is in no way essential to the homework process, it shouldn't become a source of aggravation for either of you.

SEVEN

Kindergarten and First Grade

Your child's days and nights of doing homework will probably start in either kindergarten or first grade. Although there shouldn't be a lot of homework at this stage, it's important that you and your child begin approaching homework in a positive, constructive spirit.

Kindergarten has changed since the days when you and I were five. When we started school, kindergarten was more or less a glorified nursery school. We played with blocks, listened to stories, and sang songs for a few hours in the morning or afternoon and then went home. We got the hang of going to school and were ready for real learning when we started first grade.

Nowadays, a kindergarten class may well last a full school day and the agenda is likely to be far more academic. The blocks are still there and there's plenty of time for play, but your kindergartner probably spends a certain amount of time each day learning about letters and words and working with numbers.

In first grade, learning—and, in many cases, homework—begins in earnest. The school day is probably divided into subject periods, during which students learn language arts and math skills in a more focused manner. A good teacher will tie the skill building to a broader social studies theme, but the emphasis is on skills.

How Reading Is Taught

Teachers have used a variety of techniques over the years to help children learn to read. Today, most reading programs use a smorgasbord approach that allows children to tap into the methods that suit their particular learning styles. Your child will probably be encouraged to use these four reading tools:

✎ **Phonics.** "Sounding it out" is the most popular method of teaching children to read. When children have been taught to recognize and pronounce all the letters, they are encouraged to "decode" words by making the sounds the letters make. Words like "cat" and "dog" are easier to sound out than words like "would" or "have," which aren't pronounced exactly as they are spelled.

✎ **Analogy.** Teachers help children see the connection between similar words. If your child can read the word "dog," for example, it shouldn't be hard for him to read "log." (This is why so many early readers use rhyming words to teach reading skills. Books like Dr. Seuss's *Hop on Pop* are wonderful for teaching new words by analogy.) By analogy, teachers also show children how to derive "hot" from "hop" and "top" from "tot."

✎ **Sight recognition.** In addition to teaching children to sound out words, teachers encourage them to recognize certain words by sight. Commonly used words like "the" and "and" soon become so familiar to children that they don't have to sound them out.

✎ **Context.** When a child has trouble decoding a particular word in a sentence, the teacher may encourage him to make an educated guess. Suppose your child looks at the sentence: "John ate the tasty cupcake." Perhaps he can read all the words but *tasty*. He may be able to figure out what the word is by thinking about the kinds of words that might be used to describe *cupcake*. Suppose he looks at the same sentence and finds he can't read the word *cupcake*. He may be able to figure it out by looking at the picture in the book (which shows John eating a cupcake).

Every child learns to read at his own rate. If you find that your child is lagging behind the class in picking up reading, you should certainly talk things over with his teacher. But if she reassures you that he is developing appropriately, you can be confident that he will eventually get the hang of it.

"I was really worried when Hope moved on from first to second grade, because she was only barely able to read. Her friends would come over and I'd hear them reading much harder things. But I talked to Hope's teacher and she said, 'I'm not worried about Hope. She has all the skills she needs—she can sound words out, she can identify words, and she can make intelligent guesses. One of these days she's going to blossom.'

"I stopped by that teacher's classroom the other day and told her, 'You were right.' Hope started second grade reading the simplest picture books and now (toward the end of the school year) she's reading chapter books. Somewhere along the line, something just clicked and now she's a reader."

—NELL F.

How to Help with Reading Homework

For homework, your child will probably be asked to bring books or a reader home and practice reading. He may also receive worksheets designed to encourage word recognition.

In addition to helping your child with the assignments he brings home, you can help him by encouraging his reading skills as much as possible. As he gets to be a better and better reader, his reading homework will become easier and easier.

Reading is the one skill your child will use most often throughout his educational career. Whether he's studying literature, mathematics, or science, he'll have to be able to read. The most important thing you can teach your child is that reading is fun. If he has a positive attitude toward reading, he'll want to read for pleasure and will keep an open mind when he's doing his reading homework.

Here's how you can help:

✎ **Let your child read aloud to you.** If he finds it difficult to read independently, it's fine at this early stage to allow him to read to you. Don't correct his mistakes unless he is obviously confused by them. Rather, listen patiently and give plenty of positive feedback.

✎ **Supply the words he can't get.** When your child stumbles over a word, you may want to suggest that he sound it out. This is fine to do occasionally, especially if you're pretty sure he will be able to get it right with a little extra effort. But don't slow down his reading by making him labor over a missing word. Fill in the blank for him so he can keep going. Next time he sees that word he may recognize it on his own.

✎ **Help him mark his place.** If your child has trouble following the words in a line of text, give him a small ruler or a bookmark he can hold under the line so that he reads the right words. He'll outgrow this marker as soon as he becomes a stronger reader.

✎ **Take turns reading aloud.** Your child should do his reading homework as independently as possible. But when you and he are reading for pleasure, take turns. You might alternate reading pages to each other, for example. That makes the story go faster and helps your child stick with it.

How to Encourage Reading

In addition to watching over the reading he does as homework, you'll want to encourage your child to read independently. Here's how to make sure reading is part of his daily life:

✎ **Keep on reading to your child.** Don't assume that because he's starting to read on his own he no longer needs you to read to him. Select books based on your sense of what he'll enjoy, not on what you think he "ought" to read. Read with verve and expression and stop to talk over what you've read with your child. In addition to feeding

Reading Aloud

For tips on the best way to read aloud to your child, pick up a copy of Jim Trelease's best-selling guide, *The New Read-Aloud Handbook* (Penguin). The book includes an excellent bibliography of children's books.

your child's love of reading, reading aloud to him also helps him to feel comfortable with the way the written word sounds. The more he hears you read, the more receptive he'll be to reading.

✎ **Take your child to the library.** Take your child to the library once a week and let him pick out books that interest him. Knowing the books have to go back next week will inspire you both to get them read in time. Make friends with your children's librarian; she's bound to have some good reading suggestions.

✎ **Feed your child's interests.** If he's just gotten an ant farm, he might like to read a book about ants. If he's a sports enthusiast, buy or check out of the library a book about baseball.

Join the Club!

Another good way to encourage your child's reading is to enroll him in a children's book club.

Here are some good clubs for beginning readers:

Books of My Very Own
Camp Hill, PA 17011

Children's Book-of-the-Month
    Club
Camp Hill, PA 17012

I Can Read Club
Field Publications
4343 Equity Drive
P.O. Box 16616
Columbus, OH 43216

Children's Choice Book Club
P.O. Box 984
Education Plaza
Hicksville, NY 11802

✎ **Provide books on tape.** Even before he learned to read, your child may have begun listening to recorded books on tape. Now that he's learning to read, he can really follow along while he listens. Look for tape recordings of well-written children's books or record your own versions of his favorite books.

✎ **Let him watch TV!** *Reading Rainbow* is one of the few television programs that are actually good for children. He'll enjoy watching the presentations of first-rate children's books. After he sees a program based on a particular book, try to take that book out of the library. At the video store, look for videos that are based on books. Videos that use the actual illustrations and text from the books are especially good.

How Writing Is Taught

The word *writing,* as it's used throughout elementary school, actually refers to four distinct, though interrelated, activities:

✎ **Creative writing.** Creative writing is the act of written self-expression. A child who records a made-up story or narrates a true experience is writing creatively. Many educators believe that children should be allowed to engage in this creative process without the constraints of grammar, spelling, or punctuation.

✎ **Handwriting.** Handwriting, or penmanship, is the way a child forms letters on the page. In kindergarten and first grade, children work on printing. The teacher may encourage children to draw letters in the air or in sand, or to trace them on rough sandpaper—all ways of helping kids get the "feel" of letters. And she'll probably provide lots of opportunities to practice, practice, practice those letters.

✎ **Spelling.** Educators disagree about the best way to teach children to spell. Many progressive teachers advocate "inventive spelling," an approach in which students are encouraged to write words the way they think they should be spelled. Allowing children to use inventive spelling, this theory holds, frees them to write spontaneously and creatively. Correct spelling, these educators argue, will come in time, largely as a result of reading correctly spelled words.

Far more common than inventive spelling enthusiasts are teachers who believe in spelling lists, spelling tests, and spelling bees. As early as the first grade, your child may begin bringing home lists of spelling words to memorize.

Somewhere in the middle ground are teachers who believe that there's a time and place for both inventive and traditional spelling. For instance, they may ask children to write a first draft using inventive spelling and then follow up with a second draft that corrects the misspelled words. In some schools, students are encouraged to use inventive spelling in the early grades while they become comfortable with writing. In later grades, students learn traditional spelling.

✎ **Punctuation and grammar.** By the time he leaves elementary school, your child will be expected to have mastered most of the rules of English. Again, some teachers will separate punctuation and grammar from creative writing, while others will lump them all together.

In a good program, the writing practice will be combined with reading instruction to form an integrated "language arts" program. At the early level, this means that the children will be writing and spelling words that they are simultaneously learning to read.

In kindergarten and first grade, your child's teacher may encourage him to write down his story ideas. She may allow him to communicate his ideas with pictures as well as words. She may ask the class to dictate ideas to her while she writes a story on the blackboard. The teacher will also ask the students to spend time practicing their handwriting and doing worksheets that offer handwriting and spelling practice.

Writing homework will most likely consist of short lists of spelling words and worksheets or work books designed to improve spelling and handwriting.

How You Can Help with Spelling Homework

If spelling lists start coming home from school in the first grade, chances are you'll be living with them for years to come. Each teacher has her own way of teaching children to spell. Some give worksheets and dictate sentences that incorporate spelling words on the theory that as they write the spelling words children learn to spell them.

Others simply assign the words and ask students to memorize them. In either case, there's likely to be a spelling test at the end of the week, so one way or another your child needs to learn these words.

As you show your child how to learn his spelling words, bear in mind that every child learns differently. Here is a variety of methods you can use—try several until you hit on the one that works best for your child:

✎ **Find the theme.** Teachers usually don't assign spelling words at random. Instead, they build a spelling list around a theme: all words with short *o* sounds for example—dog, log, rod, pod—or all words that end in a silent *e*—have, large, love, pave. Help your child find the theme and he'll have more power over the list.

✎ **Eliminate known words.** A long spelling list can appear daunting but chances are your child already knows how to spell some of the words. Give him a little test, in which you read off the words and have him write them down. The ones he already knows he won't need to memorize. (Have him practice them at the end of week, however, to make sure he hasn't forgotten them.) It's a satisfying feeling to cross known words off the list—let your child do this. Also, let him cross off new words as he learns them. This way, even if the last couple of words are harder to commit to memory than others, you can point out that he only has two or three left.

✎ **Have your child write down the words.** The more often he writes them correctly, the more likely he is to learn the correct spelling. Have him write one word over and over again five or six times and then move on to the next word. It may be more fun to practice typing them on a typewriter or computer.

✎ **Dictate sentences.** Make up some sentences that use the spelling words. Sometimes writing the word in context makes more sense to a child.

✎ **Use flash cards.** You may not want to use flash cards for spelling because if you do, your child will be dependent on you (or someone else in the family) to help him practice. But some children have an easier time memorizing "in their heads" than on paper, so this method may be worth a try. Have your child make up the flash cards himself on blank index cards and then you can test him. Each time you say a word, ask him to repeat the word and then spell it out loud.

Then show him the card with the spelling word so that he can read the correct spelling out loud. Discard the words he knows as he learns them, just as you would when eliminating them from a written list.

✎ **Play Spelling Concentration.** Make a second set of flash cards. Shuffle the two sets and place them face down on the table. Have your child turn over any two cards. If they match, he can put them aside. But if they don't match he should turn them back over but try to remember where they were. He should keep going until he has matched all the words. This game can be played alone or with a partner.

✎ **Give it a beat.** While some children do well with visual aids like flash cards, others have a more auditory learning style. Your child may have an easier time learning his spelling words if he claps hands (one clap per letter) as he spells so that he learns the word's rhythm. Or he may like to sing the spelling word.

✎ **Take it on the road.** Practice spelling words while you're driving, standing in line at the supermarket, or waiting for big sister to finish soccer practice.

✎ **Give a pretest.** As I discussed in Chapter 4, it's important to spread out an assignment like a spelling list over the time the teacher has allotted. The night before the classroom test, give a pretest at home. Read the words to your child and have him write them down. Then let him correct his own pretest. Allow some time for working on the words he missed.

✎ **Teach your child to test himself.** Let your child make a tape recording of the spelling list. Then he can listen to the tape and write down the words as he hears them.

How to Help Your Child with Handwriting

Just when your child has mastered the uppercase alphabet it's time for a new challenge: learning to read and write using lowercase letters. Fortunately, since reading and writing go together, your child will probably be familiar with the lowercase letters before he has to start writing them. Still, since the lowercase letters look entirely different

Ghost, Jr.

Here's a fun game for beginning spellers. One player says a word—let's say it's *cat*. The second player says a word that starts with the last letter of the first word—*top,* for example. And so on. For beginning spellers, figuring out the last letter is challenging and fun.

from capitals, learning to write lowercase is in some ways like learning from scratch.

Your child will probably be taught to write using one of two alphabets—Zaner-Bloser, which you and I probably were taught, or D'Nealian, which is a newer method. D'Nealian-printed letters are slightly slanted to the right and designed to ease the transition to cursive writing. Find out which method is being used in your child's class and try to get a copy of the appropriate alphabet. Then post the alphabet in a prominent spot in your home. Try to use this alphabet yourself when you write notes to your child.

Like so many other skills, handwriting develops over time. If your child is working hard at his handwriting but not getting very far, chances are he just needs time. If his handwriting is so sloppy that his teacher is unable to read his work, you may need to give him some extra help. Here's how:

✎ **Hold hands.** If your child has trouble forming letters, you can help him by giving him tactile experience on the letters. Hold your child's hand as he traces letters in sand, in clay, or in the air. Hold his hand while he traces giant letters in mud with a stick.

✎ **Give him letters to trace.** There are two ways to do this. You might lightly print the letters on a piece of paper and let him go over them with a darker pencil. Or you could tape a piece of tracing paper over letters you've written and have him trace them directly.

✎ **Practice, practice.** If you have your child practice good penmanship by writing out his spelling words, you'll be killing two birds with one stone. Encourage him to make his letters a uniform shape and size, with the same amount of space between the letters. Write out some sentences (using his spelling words) that he can copy. Point out the importance of leaving spaces between the words.

✎ **Fill-in-the-box method.** If uniformity of size and shape is a problem, take a sheet of triple-ruled paper and draw vertical lines down the page to mark off letter-sized squares. Have your child practice filling the squares.

How to Encourage Writing Skills

Although your child will probably not bring home writing assignments in kindergarten or first grade, you can begin to encourage his writing skills now. Here are some skill-builders you may want to try.

✎ **Encourage your child to dictate stories.** At this age, your child's verbal expressions far outstrip his ability to write down his thoughts. Let him dictate stories to you and encourage him to illustrate his stories. This will also help with reading, since he already knows his story, and will build a sense of pride and pleasure in the writing process.

✎ **Let your child make a scrapbook.** Kids are natural collectors; a scrapbook is a good way to put their "treasures" to use. After a family vacation or an interesting outing, your child might enjoy gluing his souvenirs—brochures, ticket stubs, photographs, postcards, and so on

---

Language Arts Games

Boggle Junior
Pictionary Junior
Spill and Spell

Language Arts Software

Muppet Word Book (Sunburst Communications)
Stickybear Reading (Weekly Reader Software)

—in a scrapbook. Help him to write simple captions under the items in the book.

✎ **Provide good supplies.** Your child's penmanship will improve when he has triple-ruled paper, easy-to-grip pencils, and fat markers and crayons. Talk to his teacher about whether he should have a triangular rubber pencil-holder to improve his grip.

How Math Is Taught

A good math program at the kindergarten and first-grade levels will emphasize the way numbers fit into our everyday lives rather than force children to memorize math equations. Children will learn to count, write numbers, and use numbers for specific tasks.

At first, when your child is in kindergarten, a big part of his job will be simply learning the numbers from one to ten. Whereas a three- or four-year-old may be able to recite, "one, two, three, four," and so on, he may not understand what these numbers mean. A kindergartner needs to understand what counting really is. He also needs to recognize and begin to write numerals.

Most math programs in the early grades use concrete objects (referred to technically as "manipulatives") to teach math concepts. A manipulative can be any object—a button, a coin, a cracker—that a child can use to build math understanding. Suppose I give you seven raisins and you eat three of them. How many are left? When posed in this way, the answer is much easier for a child to determine than when he's asked, "What's seven minus three?"

Many schools use a group of manipulatives called multibased blocks. These interconnecting blocks represent ones, tens, and hundreds. As children handle these objects they learn more about numbers. In the early grades, math-related tasks like sorting, classifying, measuring, and weighing are also taught.

In poorly funded or traditionally oriented school systems, teachers rely more on the old-fashioned, rote-learning approach to teaching math. Once children have learned to count and to write numbers, teachers begin training them in "math facts": $2 + 2 = 4$; $4 - 3 =$

1; and so on. If your child's teacher uses this approach, she'll probably give out worksheets for drill—both in class and as homework.

How to Help with Math Homework

Math homework in the first two grades is likely to consist of simple worksheets. When your kindergartner or first-grader brings home math homework, read the directions and make sure your child understands the homework. Here's how to help with math facts:

✎ **Make your own manipulatives.** If he's having trouble with math concepts, use your own manipulatives to help him get a better grasp of the subject. To answer the problem 3 + 4, have him line up three Legos and four Legos and count the total. To answer the problem 7 − 4, give him seven paper clips and have him take four away. Pennies, pretzels, grapes, poker chips, toothpicks, spools of thread, small building blocks, and silverware all make good manipulatives.

✎ **Flash cards.** Math flash cards are easier on parents than spelling flash cards because your child can test himself. Give him a pack of index cards and have him write out the equation (e.g., 3 + 7) on one side and the answer (e.g., 10) on the other. Then he can look at the equation, think the answer in his head, and then check the back. Just as with spelling flash cards, he can discard the cards he gets right consistently. Even though he can test himself, he may appreciate your involvement. You can also use flash cards backward. Give him the answer and ask him to come up with one of the equations that could yield that answer.

✎ **Play Math Bingo.** Draw lines on several pieces of construction paper to divide them into sixteen squares. Put the answers to math equations in the squares. Then place your flash cards, equation side up, in a stack on the table. Look at the equation on the top card and then cover the answer on your sheet (with a coin or other marker) if you have it. Discard that card and continue through the stack until someone has all his squares covered.

✎ **Play Math Concentration.** Here you make two sets of index cards, one with math problems (e.g., 2 × 7) and one with math answers (e.g., 14). Shuffle the cards and spread them out on a table.

Like other kinds of Concentration, each player turns over two cards at a time, looking for a match. Only here the "match" is the problem and its solution. When you have a match, put that pair of cards aside. Whoever has the most pairs at the end of the game wins.

✎ **Explain math relationships.** Sometimes the prospect of learning a whole set of equations can seem daunting. Help your child understand that $4 + 3$ is the same as $3 + 4$. And that $7 - 3 = 4$ is the reverse of $4 + 3 = 7$. Triangular flashcards (p. 130) are good for explaining math relationships. You might also try a version of Concentration in which congruent pairs (e.g., $6 + 3$ and $3 + 6$) are matches.

How to Encourage Math Skills

The more you help your child to feel comfortable with numbers, the more receptive he'll be to learning about math. Make math a part of your everyday life in these ways:

✎ **Encourage your young collector.** What does your child collect? Stickers? Rocks? Action figures? Coins? Children actually use the same part of their brains to work on collecting that they use for math skills. Does your child put all his fuzzy stickers on one page and all his "oilies" on another? Does your child keep National League baseball cards separate from American League cards? Sorting and classifying are important math skills. Encourage your child to organize his collection; provide the materials he needs to keep it organized—a scrapbook, an accordion file, an empty egg carton, and so on. Encourage him to keep track: He has all the Peter Pan figures except Mr. Smee and Wendy. He needs Sid Fernandez and Dwight Gooden to make his collection of Mets pitchers complete.

✎ **Throw away your dice.** When you're playing a game like Chutes and Ladders, in which you normally use dice to advance, use flash cards instead. At first, your child might carry out the operation on the card literally. For example, if the card says, "$9 - 3$," he might go forward nine spaces and back three. This is an excellent way of tying the symbolism of math into a concrete operation. As your child memorizes his math facts, he'll be able simply to move ahead six.

Number of the Day

When your child is learning his numbers, you can help by drawing a large numeral on a sheet of construction paper. Post this number on the refrigerator or another prominent place and point out that it is the "number of the day." Look for examples of the number: five raindrops on the window, five flowers in the vase, and so on. Divide your child's sandwich into five pieces or let him string five pieces of macaroni to make a necklace.

When he's ready, you can post the math fact ($4 + 5 = 9$) of the day as well.

✎ **Take your child grocery shopping.** Kids this age generally love to help out and there's lots they're able to do. Can he put the sixty-four-ounce detergent in the cart, along with a four-pack of toilet paper? Can he weigh two pounds of apples and a pound of green beans? Can he choose the medium-sized bottle of juice?

✎ **Give him your pennies.** Whenever your coin purse is overloaded with pennies, pass them on to your child. He'll be eager to spend them but first he'll need to count and organize them. You might get him some coin wrappers from the bank and show him how to package fifty pennies.

✎ **Ask him to help with organizational tasks.** When you bring the groceries home, ask him to help you put them away—fruits go in one part of the fridge, vegetables in another, canned foods on a shelf in the pantry. Or ask him to help you put away the clean laundry—shirts in one drawer, socks and underwear in another. This kind of classification helps with an understanding of mathematical categories like ones, tens, hundreds, and others.

✎ **Ask him to set the table.** Suppose Granny and Grandpa are coming to dinner. There are four of you, plus the two grandparents. How many forks, knives, and spoons will he need? As he puts one of everything at each place, he learns one-to-one correspondence.

✎ **Let him handle money.** If he has a dollar, how many packs of gum can he buy? How much change will he get back? Let him make small purchases for you so that he gets accustomed to handling money.

✎ **Talk about time.** If it's 11:30 now, he only has to wait half an hour (thirty minutes) for lunch. Although he's not ready to compute the time difference between 2:50 and 3:15, he is ready to start understanding the distance between two points in time.

✎ **Open a bank account for your child.** Let him have his own bank book and help him keep track of deposits and withdrawals.

Math Software

Math and Me (Davidson)

Math Rabbit (Learning Company)

Math Games

Guess Who

Dominoes

Uno

EIGHT

Second and Third Grades

By the time your child starts second grade, learning will have begun in earnest. Gone are the blocks, puzzles, and games that she got to play with in kindergarten and may still have had access to in the first grade. Now she's spending more and more time at her desk (or sitting with other children at a small table) doing "seat work."

In second and third grade, the school day becomes increasingly structured. In addition to continuing with language arts and math, your child will begin to experience a wider curriculum that should include social studies and science. Depending on how well the school is funded, she may also be exposed to art, music, and a foreign language.

If your child hasn't had homework up to now, she will almost certainly start getting it in second grade. This may be the time when you find you have to cut back on afterschool play to make time for homework. Most of the homework will be in math and language arts, but a creative teacher will mix in some science and social studies as well.

In second and third grade, your child may begin taking tests in various subject areas as well as in spelling. Although she may be expected to study for tests at home, the teacher may *not* tell her how to study. Imparting this valuable skill may be left up to you.

How Language Arts Are Taught

When she starts second grade, your child will probably begin working with a basal reading program. Basal (derived from the word basic) readers are textbooks that contain various short pieces of writing. Whether the reading passages are written specifically for the program or are anthologized from existing literature, the prose is written or edited for "readability." The textbook manufacturer seeks to limit vocabulary and to keep syntax at a level that the child can easily manage. Textbook manufacturers usually market entire basal programs that include workbooks, teachers' manuals, and printed worksheets.

In a good reading program, the teacher will supplement the basal reader with a variety of other books. The more individualized the reading program, the more children will be encouraged to select and read their own books.

In the second grade, reading will continue to be mostly fictional stories. But in the third grade, the reading program—or the teacher—will begin to mix in some nonfictional, factual reading as well. From now on, reading will be a way of acquiring information as well as an enjoyable pursuit.

As they did in kindergarten and first grade, children will continue to use "attack skills"—like phonics and sight recognition—as they learn to read. But toward the end of third grade, genuine mastery will begin to take over. Now, reading development will be more a matter of building a vocabulary and getting lots of reading practice, and less a matter of decoding words.

In many classrooms, the teacher divides the class into two or more reading groups, based on each child's stage of reading development. This way, groups of children can read together at the same level.

Writing continues to include the various elements described in the last chapter. The teacher will continue to drill the students in spelling, handwriting, and grammar, using workbooks and worksheets from the basal reading program.

The teacher will probably also set aside a portion of the school day for creative writing. Often, the teacher will encourage students to set down their ideas spontaneously and then ask them to edit their

The Pros and Cons of Basal Readers

Like so many other educational issues, the use of basal readers is controversial. Here are some of the arguments pro and con:

Pros:

- Basal reading programs provide an integrated approach. When the same vocabulary words are used in both text and worksheet, for example, each reinforces the other.
- These prepared materials considerably lighten the teacher's workload, leaving her free to give more individualized attention to her students.

Cons:

- When teachers stick to the basal program, they limit their students' learning experience. Children have few opportunities to experience the broader world of literature in the classroom.
- Basal readers, which are compiled by education experts, may be of much lower literary quality than picture books and novels written by creative writers. Some children may find the basals —and therefore reading in general—boring.
- The textbook manufacturers' efforts to make text "readable" are often at the expense of style and literary quality.
- The basal workbooks and worksheets are designed to address the needs of the average student—there's no room for individual variation.
- The integrated approach can turn something fresh and alive (literature) into something forced and contrived (the reading program).

drafts to correct spelling and punctuation mistakes. Depending on the particular assignment, the children may then be asked to prepare final drafts, or to read their stories out loud.

How to Help with Reading Homework

Depending on your child's reading level, she may already be reading independently by the time she starts second grade. She will almost certainly be doing so by the beginning of third grade. By all means encourage that independence. Just give her a warm, cozy, well-lit place and leave it to her. If she's having trouble keeping up with the class, here are some ways you can help:

✎ **Preread the assignment.** If you read the story ahead of time yourself, you'll be better able to help her. If there are certain words you know she's going to have trouble with, write them down and go over them before she starts reading.

✎ **Be available.** If your child still feels more comfortable reading aloud than silently, that's fine. Whether she reads to you or to herself, make yourself available to help her with words she can't read.

✎ **Ask questions.** If your child looks up after a page or two and says she doesn't understand what she's reading, ask some judicious questions. Who is the story about? What does the person (or animal) do in the story? Where does it take place? As she answers your questions, your child may find out that she knows more than she thinks. If she still doesn't get it, read the first few paragraphs to your child. Once she understands the story's premise she's more likely to understand the rest.

If your child enjoys reading, she may be tempted to read ahead in her basal reader. But it's better for her to read along with the rest of the class. There are plenty of other books she can read instead of the reader.

How to Build Reading Skills

In addition to supporting your child's classroom reading, you'll want to encourage her natural desire to read as much as possible. The goal is to make reading a pleasurable activity that your child seeks out as one of her leisure pursuits. Here are some ways you can help:

✎ **Don't throw away the "babyish" picture books your child has outgrown.** They make good primers for budding readers. Since your child has already heard the stories over and over again (and has

Finding the Right Books

How can you know which books your child is likely to enjoy? One way is to talk to your children's librarian and ask for suggestions. Ideally, she will get to know your child over time and will begin to set aside books she thinks she'll enjoy. Another option is to refer to any of several excellent bibliographies. In most cases, these bibliographies give cross indexes that tell you which books deal with specific subjects: sports, horses, historical themes, death, divorce, and so on.

For Reading Out Loud! A Guide to Sharing Books with Children by Margaret M. Kimmel and Elizabeth Segel (Dell)

Best Books for Children: Preschool through Grade 6 by John T. Gillespie and Corinne J. Naden (Bowker)

Fantasy Literature for Children and Young Adults by Ruth N. Lynn (Bowker)

A to Zoo: Subject Access to Children's Picture Books by Carolyn W. Lima and John A. Lima (Bowker)

The New York Times *Parent's Guide to the Best Books for Children* by Eden R. Lipson (Random House)

You might also consider enrolling your child in the Weekly Reader Book Club (Field Publications, 4343 Equity Drive, P.O. Box 16616, Columbus, Ohio 43216), which carries excellent titles for children aged four to twelve.

probably memorized some), it won't be hard for her to decode these old favorites. The feeling of accomplishment she'll derive from reading the books that used to be read to her will give her the confidence to tackle harder books.

✎ **On the other hand, don't be afraid to supply more sophisticated books.** If your child happens to be a stronger reader than her classmates, she should have the opportunity to tackle more challenging material.

✎ **Enlist your child as a reader.** Ask your child to read to her younger sister or brother. Or seek out other younger children to whom your child can read.

✎ **Let your child record a book.** Reading is more interesting when you can record yourself doing it. Your child might enjoy making a "books on tape" recording for a younger child, complete with a suitable noise that indicates that the listener should turn the page.

✎ **When you eat out, encourage your child to read her own menu.** There's a wonderful feeling of competence that comes from making your own decisions in a restaurant.

✎ **Allow "junk" reading.** The more your child enjoys reading the more likely she is to become a strong reader. It's better for her to read two "low art" books she likes than one "classic" that she has to slog through unwillingly. Allow your child to read comic books, mysteries, series novels, and any other appropriate material that interests her.

✎ **When you go grocery shopping, give your child your shopping list and ask her to find the items on the list.** Use this trick for other lists, too. You might make a list of all the errands you have to run today and have her check off the tasks as they are completed.

✎ **Make a treasure hunt.** Here's a fun reason to read. Hide a small object somewhere in your house. Make a series of clues, each leading to the next, that your child can follow to find the missing object. The first clue might read, for example, "Look in the refrigerator." Inside the 'fridge your child might find a second clue, "Look in your sweater drawer," and so on. For more advanced readers, try harder clues: "If you want a nice cool drink, take a look in the kitchen _____."

✎ **Ham it up!** Another way to encourage reading is to give your child and her friends a script and let them perform a small skit or play. They'll have so much fun they'll hardly notice they're reading! You

The In-Between Reader

Between the time your child is still reading picture books and the time when she is able to read full-length novels, you may find you have a hard time finding books that are neither too babyish nor too challenging. There are a number of book series aimed directly at your in-between reader. These books have the satisfying look and feel of novels but offer simple texts and plenty of illustrations.

The Kids of the Polk Street School series by Patricia R. Giff (Dell)

Nate the Great series by Marjorie Weinman Sharmat (Dell Yearling)

Frog and Toad books by Arnold Lobel (Harper and Row)

Little Bear books by Else Homelund Minarik (Harper and Row)

The Littles series by John Peterson (Scholastic)

Cam Jansen series by David A. Adler (Puffin, Dell, Viking)

The Baby-Sitters Little Sister series by Ann M. Martin (Scholastic)

Two Judy Blume titles also make great in-between reading. They are: *The One in the Middle is the Green Kangaroo* (Dell) and *Freckle Juice* (Dell).

can make up your own play together or find a published play. Check with your children's librarian to see if she has any appropriate plays, or write to Baker's Plays, 100 Chauncy Street, Boston, Massachusetts 02111, for a catalog that includes many children's plays and musicals.

✎ **Provide nonfiction books.** Some children aren't particularly interested in reading fiction. If your child doesn't care for novels, you'll be hard pressed to get her to read them for pleasure. But kids who don't like fiction are often intensely interested in other reading. Does your child love animals? You can probably find books about all kinds of animals at the library. Is she an ardent skater? Buy or borrow a book about skating.

✎ **Be a good role model.** Show your child that you consider reading worthwhile by doing plenty of your own reading. If you're not in

Drama Fun

Here's a great party game that draws on reading skills. Divide the children into pairs or threes. Give each group a set of written instructions. For example: "You are acting out 'Snow White.' One of you is Snow White and the other is the wicked queen. Act out the scene in which the queen disguises herself and persuades Snow White to eat the poison apple." Send each group off to rehearse. Tell them to "act out" the story without words. When everyone comes back, let the others guess what scene each group is performing.

The Ultimate Inducement: Staying Up Late

Here's a surefire way to induce your child to read. Tell her that she can stay up an extra half-hour if she spends the time reading in bed!

the habit of reading already, you don't have to embark on a "great novels" course. Turn off the TV and read the newspaper, a magazine, or a juicy bestseller.

How to Help Your Child with Language Arts Worksheets

Even if your child didn't bring home any worksheets in the first grade, she's almost certain to start bringing them home now. The first few worksheets can be daunting, so help your child develop a system for doing them.

Here's how:

✎ **Read the instructions aloud.** There's a good chance that the child who wails, "I don't get it!" upon first viewing her worksheet hasn't read the instructions. When you ask if she's read the instructions, she may say yes but what she really means is that she has quickly scanned the directions and then looked at the confusing material underneath the directions that constitutes the worksheet itself. She can't get away with this if she reads the directions aloud.

In many cases, as she reads aloud you may be almost able to see the light bulb turning on over her head as she utters a relieved, "Oh, I get it now." Let her read the directions aloud to you the first few times she has worksheets, then teach her to read them aloud to herself.

✎ **Make sure she understands the directions.** If you think she should be able to understand the directions, try to help her come to an understanding of them without simply telling her what to do. Have her break the directions into parts. Which part doesn't she understand? What does she think it could possibly mean? Are there several parts to the instructions? If so, it may help her to number the steps she has to take.

Why not just explain what to do? After all, isn't her task to do the exercises, not read the instructions? Yes and no. Reading, understanding and executing written directions like these will be a part of her educational career for many years to come. You want her to get used to the way these instructions are written and to take responsibility for interpreting them.

On the other hand, some directions are genuinely confusing. On a number of occasions when my daughter has had trouble understanding the directions on a worksheet, I've found that I'm just as unable to decipher the author's intent as she is. Several times we've called in my husband for a third opinion, but sometimes we're all left guessing. Teachers are fallible and so are the publishers who mass-produce worksheets. If the directions are genuinely difficult, explain the instructions to your child in your own words. You might send a note to the teacher about your confusion.

✎ **Look at the questions.** Once your child has read the directions, her next move is to look at the problems on the worksheet. With luck, there will be a sample question that has already been answered. If not, she'll have to look at the first few problems and think, "How can I apply the directions I've been given to the problems on this sheet?" If your child continues to be baffled, it may be that she hasn't understood the classroom lesson that preceded this homework assignment. Now you'll have to decide whether to let her bring the homework back unanswered or to try to teach her the material that's been covered.

How to Help with Cursive Writing

Sometime around the third or fourth grade, your child will begin to learn how to write in cursive. If she's been using the D'Nealian alphabet, this will be simply a matter of learning how to connect the letters into script. If she's been using the traditional Zaner-Bloser alphabet, she'll have to learn from the ground up, but so many of the letters are similar that learning cursive should still be easier than learning to print was.

Here's how you can help:

✎ **Compliment her on her progress.** Writing in cursive is a major developmental step and most children are excited about making this transition. Draw on that excitement to provide positive reinforcement. Feeling "big" may compensate for the drudgery of doing worksheets.

✎ **Provide inviting materials.** Ruled paper will make it easier to keep cursive writing even, but colored ruled paper will make it more fun. Thin-tipped markers feel nice as they move across the page and make satisfyingly elegant letters.

✎ **Provide writing samples.** As you did when she was learning to print, post samples of the handwriting style your child's teacher is aiming for. Write out sentences for her to copy, using the week's spelling words.

✎ **Help her form the letters correctly.** As you did when she learned to print, you may want to make vertical lines on her page to help her give her letters the right size and shape. You might also lightly pencil in a slanted line in each box to remind your child to write on an angle.

✎ **Consider calligraphy.** If your child is interested, you might let her take a calligraphy class. The approach is quite different from cursive writing, but it's almost sure to result in neater, more attractive penmanship.

✎ **Or . . . teach her to type.** It's important for your child to learn cursive writing. But it's also important that her teachers be able to read her essays and other written assignments. With the teacher's permission, teach your child to type and let her type or word-process some of her written work. It will be a relief to her to be able to write

Hangman

What's fun, educational, and requires only a pencil and paper? You guessed, it's your old friend Hangman. Use the week's spelling words and help your child practice them.

In case you've forgotten, here's how to play. Draw a gallows and hangman's noose. Decide what word you want your child to spell and make as many blank spaces as there are letters in the word. Now your child guesses letters. If she gets a letter that's in the word, you put it in the appropriate space. But if the letter isn't in the word, you write it on the side and begin drawing the hanging victim. If your child comes up with the word before you've drawn the entire victim, she wins. If you draw the victim first, she loses. Give your child the chance to draw the hangman while you guess, too.

If you have a computer, you may want to purchase a Hangman game. Choose one that allows your child to enter the week's spelling list.

without worrying about her handwriting, and typing may give her more freedom of creative expression.

How to Build Writing Skills

At this stage, writing homework, if there is any, is likely to consist mostly of sentences and short paragraphs. (If your child is getting

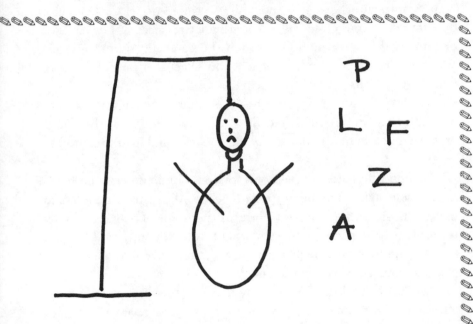

P.S. At the Quaker school my daughter attends, Hangman is considered too violent, so the children play Spider. You start with a big circle for the body and add legs, head, and features.

longer assignments, read the section on writing in the next chapter.) You can help prepare your child for longer assignments by encouraging her to write at home. Here are some fun projects that will keep her pen flowing.

✎ **Encourage letter writing.** Help your child get in the habit of corresponding with friends and family members. Interesting stationery supplies, neat-colored markers, and stickers will make letter writing more inviting. As a birthday present, you might give her an ink pad and a stamp with her name and address printed on it. Or buy her a date stamp. If your child balks at writing letters, let her buy cards or preprinted thank-you notes on which she can send short messages. When you're on vacation, let your child select postcards to send to family and friends.

✎ **Brag a little.** Let your child know how much you like her writing by posting her most recent writing assignment on the 'fridge or elsewhere around the house. Or make copies and mail them to her relatives.

✎ **Fun with notes.** Leave notes for your child and encourage her to send you some. You might put a blackboard or erasable cardboard bulletin board in a prominent place in the house. Encourage family members to send messages to each other through "family mail." Write a riddle or a joke on a small scrap of paper and leave it at your child's place; encourage her to do the same.

✎ **Post a list.** Keep your grocery list and other lists posted on the refrigerator or in some other prominent spot. Encourage your child to write extra entries on the lists.

How Math Is Taught

Remember "new math"? Well, it's old now. New math, which you and I learned, was supposed to deemphasize rote learning in favor of teaching the broader concepts of mathematics. Unfortunately, this emphasis on conceptualization left students confused about the ways in which math ideas apply to actual math problems.

Today the way math is taught varies considerably from school to

Language Arts Games

Clue Jr.
Scrabble for Juniors
Trivial Pursuit for Juniors

Language Arts Software

Bank Street Writer Plus (Broderbund Software)
Writer Rabbit (Learning Company)

school. In many schools, the approach is back to rote learning, with an emphasis on "math facts" like $5 \times 7 = 35$. In other classrooms, the emphasis is on practical applications: How tall is the classroom? What temperature is it today? How does that compare with yesterday's temperature?

Children in the early primary grades still need plenty of opportunities to link the ideas they're learning to the concrete reality these ideas express. For example, seeing five sets of seven blocks will help them understand what $5 \times 7 = 35$ *means*. They should continue to use multibased blocks and other devices.

During these grades, your child will probably spend time identifying and playing with various shapes. Later on, this involvement with shapes will emerge into geometry.

By the end of third grade, your child will probably be expected to have mastered all the "math facts": that is, every addition and subtraction problem from $1 + 1 = 2$ $(2 - 1 = 1)$ through $10 + 10 = 20$ $(20 - 10 = 10)$ and every multiplication and division problem from $1 \times 1 = 1$ $(1 \div 1 = 1)$ through $10 \times 10 = 100$ $(100 \div 10 = 10)$.

In addition to memorizing math facts, your child will be taught to perform more complex operations, such as carrying in addition problems and borrowing in subtraction problems. She'll begin to work with the concepts of greater than ($>$) and less than ($<$).

Counting continues to be part of the math curriculum. Although it might seem to you that a child who can borrow and carry and otherwise seems comfortable with numbers will naturally be able to count beyond one hundred, the truth is that counting can be difficult. Learning place value—recognizing, for example, that the number 3456 means three thousand four hundred and fifty-six—takes time and effort.

During third grade, your child will probably encounter fractions for the first time. She may begin to add and subtract fractions, but for now she will probably only get problems in which the denominator (the bottom number) stays the same: $\frac{1}{2} + \frac{1}{2}$, for example.

In measuring, your child may learn both the metric and the English system. Your child will begin learning to estimate. And she'll also work with time and money measurement.

Each teacher has her own way of teaching math, and you and your child will need to conform to the approach your child's teacher uses. You may do more harm than good by trying to impart your own methods to your child. As you help her do her homework, try to respect the teacher's approach and teach your child to function within that method.

As with language arts, the teacher may divide students into math groups and help each group advance at its own speed.

How to Help Your Child with Math Homework

The process of learning math skills is cumulative. Each new task builds on one or more tasks that went before. Simple addition, for example, builds on counting. Complex addition, involving carrying, builds on the simple addition facts learned previously. Perhaps more than in any other area of her education, it's vital that your child keep up with what's being taught.

If your child has kept up, she probably won't have much trouble understanding her math homework. By the time she brings home an assignment involving carrying, for example, she should have successfully worked many similar math problems at school. If your child doesn't understand the homework, it may be that she hasn't under-

Quick! What's a Quotient?

If it's been a while since you were in the third grade (and I assume it has been), you've probably forgotten those nifty words that mean the number that you add to the other number, or the number that you get when you divide the first number. Since your child will be learning these terms, it's a good idea for you to learn them again too. Here they are:

$$22 \leftarrow \text{addend}$$
$$+45 \leftarrow \text{addend}$$
$$67 \leftarrow \text{sum}$$

$$67 \leftarrow \text{minuend}$$
$$-45 \leftarrow \text{subtrahend}$$
$$22 \leftarrow \text{difference}$$

$$45 \leftarrow \text{factor}$$
$$\times 11 \leftarrow \text{factor}$$
$$55$$
$$44$$
$$495 \leftarrow \text{product}$$

$$45 \leftarrow \text{quotient}$$
$$11 \overline{)496} \leftarrow \text{dividend}$$
divisor $\nearrow$
$$44$$
$$56$$
$$55$$
$$1 \leftarrow \text{remainder}$$

stood the lesson on carrying that was given in class. It's just as likely, however, that she didn't really have a firm grasp on simple addition when complex addition was introduced.

Often, then, the best way to help your child with math homework is to review and practice the steps leading up to the current skill. It's worth spending extra time, perhaps on the weekend, working with your child to help her stay on track with the rest of the class. (See pp. 63–65.)

Here are some tips for helping your child tackle some specific kinds of problems.

Math Matters

The National PTA is aware of the problems many children have with math and the need for greater parent involvement. It has devised a program called Math Matters, designed to help local PTAs educate and assist parents. If you're interested in finding out more about this program, write to The National PTA, 700 North Rush Street, Chicago, Illinois 60611.

Borrowing and Carrying

There are two main ways in which borrowing and carrying can pose a problem. The first is conceptual: your child may just not "get" the idea behind these two operations. To help with this problem, return to concrete physical explanations. Suppose she's adding 27 + 34. Use two sets of manipulatives to represent the tens and ones. Let's say you're using poker chips. You'll need two blue and seven red chips for 27 and three blue and four red chips for 34. How many red chips are there? 11. Trade ten of those eleven into the bank for one blue and one red chip. Now "carry" that extra blue chip over to the other blue chips to make six blue chips. The answer: six blues and a red = 61. Go back to the numbers and show how to do the same thing on paper.

The second problem has to do with neatness. Unless your child happens to be naturally meticulous, she will find it difficult to learn to keep straight which numbers are changing, which are being borrowed or carried, and so on. It will help if you let your child work out each problem on a large section of paper. Wide-ruled graph paper works very well. If the teacher's method includes crossing out and changing numerals, show your child how to do this in the graph square above where the original number is.

Show your child how to check her own math problems. Subtraction and addition are, of course, the reverse of one another, so show her how to check her answers by reversing the operation. For example:

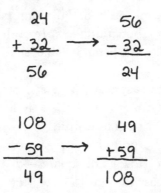

For most people, subtraction is a little harder than addition. Borrowing from 0 is especially tricky. Let's say the problem is 406 − 99. You can't subtract 9 from 6, so six needs to borrow 1 from 0 to make it 16. But you can't borrow from 0, since 0 is nothing. So you have to borrow from 40. Borrowing 1 from 40 makes it 39. Make sure your child changes both digits (the 4 and the 0) before she proceeds with the problem.

$$
\begin{array}{r}
\overset{3\ \ 9}{4\,0\,6} \\
-\ 9\,9 \\
\hline
3\,0\,7
\end{array}
$$

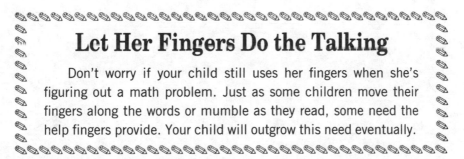

Let Her Fingers Do the Talking

Don't worry if your child still uses her fingers when she's figuring out a math problem. Just as some children move their fingers along the words or mumble as they read, some need the help fingers provide. Your child will outgrow this need eventually.

Multiplication and Division Facts

Memorizing the multiplication and division tables is much like memorizing addition and subtraction facts. In both cases, it's important to make sure your child understands what she's memorizing. Here are some strategies:

✎ **Eliminate the easy ones.** You can help by encouraging your child to get the easy ones out of the way first. Your child probably won't have too much trouble learning the 2 and 3 times tables. 10s are easy and so are 5s. 6s and 9s are easy if you teach your child the easy methods. (See p. 131.) The squares—2 × 2, 3 × 3, 4 × 4, and so on—tend to be easy for kids to learn, too. By the time she learns all the "easy" facts, there won't be all that many "hard" ones left!

✎ **Make a multiplication chart.** On a sheet of graph paper, have your child write the numbers from one to ten across the top and again down the side. Have her fill in the multiples of these numbers in the squares. Now have her work with flash cards every night. At the end of each session, set aside the math facts she's learned. Now have her fill in the corresponding boxes with colored markers. As the unshaded area shrinks, she'll see she has less and less to learn. (See p. 132.)

✎ **Use triangular flash cards.** Cut some index cards into triangles. Put each of the components of a multiplication problem in one corner of each card.

This card actually represents four equations: 5 × 6 = 30; 6 × 5 = 30; 30 ÷ 6 = 5; and 30 ÷ 5 = 6. Have your child look at the

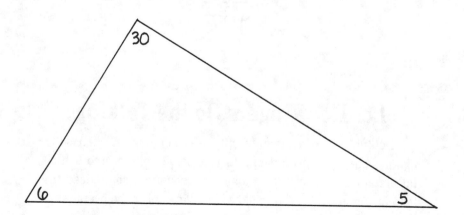

Easy 6s and 9s

Here's how to make learning the 6 and 9 times tables a breeze!

6s:

Let's say the equation is 4×6. What's 4×5? 20. Just add one more 4 and you get 24. How about 7×6? $7 \times 5 = 35$. Just one more 7 is 42. All your child has to do is multiply the other number by five and then add one more of the first number.

9s:

What's 9×8? 10×8 is easy, right? So what's one less 8? 72. How about 9×4? $10 \times 4 = 40$. One less four is 36. All your child has to do is multiply the other number by ten and then take away one less of the first number.

card and say all four equations. Not only will this reinforce math facts but it will also help your child see how these math facts are interrelated. (You can also use triangular flash cards for addition and subtraction math facts.)

How to Build Math Skills

You'd be surprised—and so might your child—to discover how often we use math skills in everyday life. Here are some ways to encourage your child to use her math skills:

✎ **Let her keep score.** When you're playing stickball or badminton in the back yard, or Gin Rummy or Uno in the living room, let your child keep score. The simple counting and adding involved is excellent practice.

✎ **Play Buzz.** This is a good car game. Choose a number, say 4. Each person in the car, in turn, counts aloud. When you reach 4 or

	1	2	3	4	5	6	7	8	9	10
1	1	2	3	4	5	6	7	8	9	10
2	2	4	6	8	10	12	14	16	18	20
3	3	6	9	12	15	18	21	24	27	30
4	4	8	12	16	20	24	28	32	36	40
5	5	10	15	20	25	30	35	40	45	50
6	6	12	18	24	30	36	42	48	54	60
7	7	14	21	28	35	42	49	56	63	70
8	8	16	24	32	40	48	56	64	72	80
9	9	18	27	36	45	54	63	72	81	90
10	10	20	30	40	50	60	70	80	90	100

Boogie Down Math

For a different approach to learning times tables, order this video for your child:

Multiplication Rock, Golden Book Videos, c/o Western Publishing, 1220 Mound Avenue, Racine, WI 53404

What about Using a Calculator?

In this age of calculators and sophisticated computer programs, does anyone really need to learn math facts? I'm afraid so. By learning her math facts, your child will come to understand the concepts underlying sophisticated mathematical equations. Furthermore, we all use math facts in our daily lives whether we own calculators or not. How would it be if you had to whip out a calculator when you wanted to add up the value of the change in your pocket? What if you needed a calculator to figure out how many yards of fabric to buy to cover a six-foot-long couch? Just as you need to be able to write with a pen even though you may use a typewriter or computer, so you need to be able to add, subtract, multiply, and divide even though you can use a calculator—and so does your child.

Another problem with calculators is that they seem to be foolproof when they really are not. It's all too easy to punch in the wrong numbers and come up with a completely wrong answer. If your child is using a calculator for fun, encourage her to make an estimate first. Then if her answer is way off the mark, she can check to be sure she entered the right figures.

As long as the calculator isn't replacing memorized math facts, there's no harm in giving your child a calculator and teaching her how to use it. Most kids enjoy using a calculator and practicing equations on a calculator will enhance your child's mathematical skill. With the teacher's permission, you might encourage your child to check her math problems with the calculator. If she gets a problem wrong, make sure she reworks it by hand.

its multiples, you say, "buzz." The next person has to say the following number. Here's how it works: Mom: 1. Dad: 2. Frank: 3. Sally: buzz. Jeff: 5. Mom: 6. Dad: 7. Frank: buzz. Sally: 9. And so on. It's harder than it sounds and a great way to learn the multiplication tables.

✏ **Let your child clip coupons.** When you go grocery shopping, your child can compare the savings the coupons offer against the prices of other brands of the same products. If she saves money, let her keep the change!

✏ **Give her her allowance in coins.** Most kids are intensely interested in the amount of their allowance. Give it to her in coins—a combination of quarters, dimes, nickels, and pennies—and tell her to add them up to make sure you gave her the right amount.

✏ **Math in the kitchen.** Cooking provides an excellent opportunity for practicing math skills. Suppose you have to double your macaroni salad recipe for the school's potluck dinner? What's twice ⅔ of a cup of sour cream? What's twice two celery stalks? What if you want to cut your lasagna recipe in half? What's half of 8 ounces of mozzarella cheese? Half of two eggs? Half of half a pound of hamburger meat?

✏ **Give her a clock or a watch.** She's old enough now to really understand what time is all about. Give her a clock in her room and teach her to be responsible about time. For example, tell her that if she's in bed by 8:15, she can read in bed until 8:45. Once she's able to tell time, let her have her own watch.

Family Math

Family Math is an exciting and innovative program developed at the Lawrence Hall of Science at the University of California, Berkeley. The program is designed to help parents and children become comfortable with math. By playing games together, everyone who participates builds math skills and overcomes math anxiety. You can order a copy of *Family Math,* the book, by Jean Kerr Stenmark, Virginia Thompson, and Ruth Cossey, from the Lawrence Hall of Science, University of California, Berkeley, California, 94720. The book is filled with games you can play with your child, and also describes how to set up a family math program in your community.

Math Books

Anno's Math Games and *Anno's Math Games II* by Mitsumasa
   Anno (Philomel)
Making Cents: Every Kid's Guide to Money by Elizabeth Wilkinson
   (Little, Brown)

Math Games

Connect Four
Parcheesi
'Smath

Math Software

Stickybear Math (Weekly Reader Software)
Math Shop Junior (Scholastic Family Software)

How Social Studies Is Taught

What *is* social studies, anyway? Years ago, before you and I were
students, social studies was history. Children learned when Caesar
conquered Gaul, the names of Columbus's ships, the dates of every
major American war to the present, and the names of every U.S.
president. As in every other subject, there was a good deal of memorization and not much theorizing.

Social studies grew out of history in an attempt to encompass
other social sciences—anthropology, political science, economics,
sociology, and so on. In many school districts, social studies take the
form of an ever-expanding self-examination. Kindergartners, for ex-

ample, might study themselves and their families. First-graders might study their neighborhoods, second-graders the community, and so on.

In more traditional school systems, the emphasis is still basically historical. Through a series of textbooks, children learn how their state was formed and developed and how America was colonized, politicized, and industrialized.

Although social studies certainly belongs in the curriculum of any well-organized elementary school class, it often gets short shrift. Your child may or may not have a social studies textbook, which may or may not be well-written and interesting.

Ideally, social studies will be interwoven into the fabric of the class's other studies. A unit about your community, for example, might generate a list of spelling words, as well as stimulate mathematical skills with projects like making a map of the immediate neighborhood.

How to Help with Social Studies Homework

Social studies homework will probably consist of answering questions based on reading and classroom discussion. The teacher may create a worksheet (or give a social studies workbook assignment) that quizzes children on the information they've learned.

If your child will have to take a test on her social studies knowledge, use the test-taking strategies below to help her prepare (see pages 140–143). Even if you consider the textbook boring and outdated, it's probably best to keep your feelings to yourself. Instead, talk to your child about her reactions to the events described in the text.

If the social studies program is more creative, your child will bring home interesting assignments, such as making a family tree, writing about her community, or making a diorama based on the information she's learned in class. Help her compile the materials she needs, but make sure the project itself is her own.

How to Encourage Social Studies

Every day you have conversations with your child that expand her knowledge of social studies. Your child's natural curiosity drives her to ask hundreds of questions about the world around her. As you answer her questions, think about your role as a teacher. Don't give long-winded or didactic answers, but do take the time to answer her fully. And ask her questions that make her think. Here are examples of the kinds of discussions that expand your child's knowledge:

✎ **Watch people at work.** What is the waitress's job at your local coffee shop? What does a lawyer do? What kind of work do Mom and Dad do? What kind of work do politicians do? What are the names of the politicians in your area?

✎ **Talk about systems.** How do the people in your neighborhood get to work? Do they travel by car, on a network of roads? Do they take public transportation? Do they walk? What are sidewalks for? Why are they higher than the street? How long does the light stay green? Why not longer? Or shorter?

These days, kids hear about a lot of topics you might prefer they didn't have to know about yet. Just what is this sexual harassment Anita Hill says Clarence Thomas committed? What causes AIDS? How did Magic Johnson get it? What did your neighbor mean when she said that the people living on the street outside your door were "released from mental institutions"? It's best not to try to sweep this kind of information under the rug. Talk to your child at a level you feel she's ready to understand.

How Science Is Taught

Like social studies, science is a vital academic subject that too often is ignored or mishandled. Again, your child may bring home a science textbook that, unfortunately, could represent the first stage of a life-long antipathy toward science.

Ideally, however, the school will offer your child lots of hands-on opportunities to experience science directly. A good science program

Social Studies Reading

It's hard to find good historical books for this age group. Here are a few books that will educate and entertain your child:

In the Year of the Boar and Jackie Robinson by Bette Bao Lord (Harper)—Chinese immigrant experience.

And Then What Happened, Paul Revere? by Jean Fritz (Coward)

The Courage of Sarah Noble by Alice Dalgliesh (Macmillan)—pioneer girl

will include observation, experimentation, and some kind of record keeping.

In the early grades, if there is any science homework, it is likely to come in the form of a special project. Your child might be asked to study a particular animal or environment, or present an experiment to the class. As you guide your child through a project of this kind, try to make sure that the project is manageable, so that she can do a good and satisfying job. If she takes on more than she can really handle, she's likely to come away feeling dissatisfied.

How to Build Science Skills

Like social studies, science is so much a part of the world around us that opportunities to discuss science and to engage in hands-on scientific experiences abound. Here are just a few ways that you can introduce your child to science. As you do these kinds of activities with your child, you do more than just increase her store of information. You are also helping her to feel good about science. Particularly if your child is a girl, you'll go a long way toward combating an antiscience bias she may encounter later in life.

   ✎ **Go take a hike.** The natural world abounds with science lessons. Just learning the names of trees and wildflowers is a good science lesson as well as a vocabulary lesson. Many state parks and wildlife sanctuaries offer numbered nature walks. You'll be given a guide and can stop at numbered markers to note sights of interest.

✎ **Bird watching.** Hang a bird feeder outside your child's window. Give her a simple guide to birds and help her identify the ones that come to her window.

✎ **Tend your own garden.** If you're into gardening, by all means include your child. Explain how sunlight, warmth, and water affect the plants you grow. Give your child her own section of the garden to tend. If you live in an apartment, give your child a houseplant to look after. Or let her grow a plant from seeds. Or give her a clipping she can sprout in water and then plant. Visit a health food store and buy a special jar to grow bean or alfalfa sprouts.

✎ **Start an aquarium or insect collection.** In an aquarium, your child can keep fish and coordinate plant life to create a good environment for her pets. Nature stores sell bug boxes for collecting insects.

✎ **Talk about the weather.** What are the people outside wearing today? Why? Check the thermometer to see what the temperature is. What season is it now? Is this weather typical of the season? What clothes will your child wear today? Why? What is the weather like in other parts of the country? In other parts of the world? Did your child know that when it's summer here it's winter in Australia?

✎ **Visit science museums.** You may want to consult *Doing Children's Museums* by Joanne Cleaver (Williamson). Many children's museums have a scientific orientation.

✎ **Read all about it.** Take a trip to the library to find books about science. Look for Joanna Coles's Magic School Bus series—titles include *The Magic School Bus inside the Earth* and *The Magic School Bus Lost in the Solar System* (Scholastic).

How Tests Are Given

Now that your child is in second or third grade, she's likely to begin taking tests on a regular basis. There may be spelling tests, math tests, or social studies or science tests. The frequency and importance of these tests depends on the teacher. Some teachers use test results as a barometer to determine how much information the class has absorbed. Others use tests as a way of rating and grading each individual student's progress.

In addition to the teacher's tests, your child will also have to take a series of standardized tests. These tests, which are given in a massive quantity to students all over the country, are designed to rate an individual's performance relative to that of her peers nationwide, and also to track the success of education in general.

"Criterion-referenced" standardized tests are provided by textbook manufacturers and used to test students' success in absorbing a given portion of the language arts or math text. "Norm-referenced" standardized tests—like the Iowa Test of Basic Skills and the Stanford Achievement Test—are long, multipart "fill in the bubble" tests designed to test students' knowledge in a range of subject areas.

Manufacturers of standardized tests frequently claim that there is no way to study for these tests. So far as elementary school students are concerned, this is probably true. The best parents can do is play the tests down and avoid putting pressure on their children to perform well. If your child is nervous about taking standardized tests, reassure her that, in the first place, the test results will not affect her grade in the classroom and, in the second place, you will love her just the same no matter how well she does. That said, encourage her to do her best but to try not to worry. Refer to the "Test Anxiety" section, pp. 142–143.

How to Study for Tests

Unlike standardized tests, tests given in the classroom by the teacher can and should be studied for. Here are some hints for helping your child learn to study for tests:

✎ **Plan ahead.** Question: When isn't the best time to start studying for a test? Answer: The night before. As soon as your child hears that there's going to be a test, she should map out a schedule for studying. (See the organizational strategies in Chapter 4.)

✎ **Make sure your child knows what she has to study.** As I've said, teachers often assume that children know more about studying than they do. Look over the assignment with your child and point out what she needs to know.

✎ **Practice answering questions.** Some textbooks give discussion questions at the end of each chapter. Your child should think about how she would answer those questions. If there are no questions, she should try to come up with her own, to anticipate the questions her teacher may ask.

✎ **Rhyme it!** When your child has to remember information, encourage her to come up with a rhyme that makes the information easier to recall. A classic example of this approach is "In fourteen hundred and ninety-two, Columbus sailed the ocean blue." Mary Thomas, a teacher in DeBery, Florida, comments, "Kids can come up with some pretty off-color rhymes. But as long as they're not too bad, I let them go—whatever helps them learn is okay with me."

✎ **Picture it!** Your child might use any of several visualization techniques to memorize information. For example, ask her to picture a particular place in her mind—her room, her favorite restaurant, her aunt and uncle's back yard, and so on. Then ask her to put the information she's studying in that place. For example, she might imagine the *Nina,* the *Pinta,* and the *Santa Maria* sailing across her bedroom rug, while Queen Isabella and King Ferdinand wave goodbye from her bed.

✎ **Think of it!** Show your child how to make personalized connections. Her favorite dinner, pineapple-baked ham, might remind her of Alexander Hamilton, while her best friend's older brother Jeff could remind her of Thomas Jefferson. Funny or outlandish catch phrases are great: Did Washington remember to wash behind his ears, George?

✎ **Talk to your child about test-taking strategies.** When the test begins, she should listen to what the teacher has to say. There may be some important piece of information she doesn't want to miss. Then she should read the directions carefully. She might be asked to answer three out of five questions—but if she doesn't read the directions she could wind up rushing through all five. Remind her to keep track of time. If she is having a lot of trouble with one question, she should move on to others, then come back to the tough one if there's time.

✎ **Make sure she gets a good night's sleep.** Don't let your child stay up late studying for the big test. Make sure she stops and gets to bed at a reasonable time. In the morning, see that she eats a nutritious breakfast.

Test Anxiety

Many people of all ages feel anxious when they're called upon to perform under pressure. That word you know perfectly well may completely slip your mind when you're playing Scrabble. You might be an expert driver except on the day when you're applying for your license.

A person who is experiencing performance anxiety may start to sweat, get a stomachache, pant, and feel a sense of panic and impending doom. If your child is prone to performance anxiety, tests can pose a terrific strain. Test anxiety makes it hard for her to concentrate and do her best. Her fears can become a self-fulfilling prophecy if she becomes so panicked that she can't remember the information she studied last night.

Fortunately, there are ways to combat test anxiety. Here are some techniques you can teach your child:

✎ **Make sure to study.** The better prepared your child is when she goes to take the test, the more confident she'll feel. Studying the material over several days will be more effective than cramming at the last minute.

✎ **Give yourself a practice test.** Tell your child to think about the kinds of questions the teacher is likely to ask. At home, where she doesn't feel pressured, she'll probably be able to think of good answers. If she's lucky, her questions will be similar enough to the ones the teacher actually asks so that she'll have a leg up on giving the answers. If the test is a straightforward spelling or math test, you may be able to make up a practice test for her.

✎ **Take deep breaths.** When she sits down to take the test, your child may experience the symptoms of panic described here. Tell her to take a moment to calm herself down. She should take five or six deep breaths, counting to herself (1–2–3–4–5) as she slowly inhales and slowly exhales.

✎ **Read the directions carefully.** See the suggestions given on pages 140–142 for test preparation.

✎ **Skip over hard questions.** Tell your child to answer the questions she feels most confident about first. This way, she has a good chance of producing some right answers, even if she runs out of time. And with those questions out of the way and plenty of time left over, she'll feel less panicky about answering the harder ones.

✎ **Keep things in perspective.** Your attitude about test taking can make a big difference. Of course you want her to do well and you don't want to let her off the hook by telling her that tests don't matter. But you do want her to feel that you sympathize with her difficulty.

Your child's anxiety is closely tied to a fear of failure. As her parent, you are intertwined in her unconscious mind with her sense of responsibility. Tell her clearly and plainly, "It's only a test. I want you to do your best but I'm not going to be angry if you fail." Suggest that she say something similar to herself: "It's only a test. I'm going to do my best and that will be good enough."

How to Build Study and Thinking Skills

Studying is very different from watching TV, playing spontaneously, or even reading for pleasure. To study successfully your child must be able to devote a concentrated period of time to one narrowly defined topic. Here are some ways you can help build your child's attention span and level of concentration.

✎ **Play "I packed a trunk to China."** Here's how the game works: The first player says, "I packed a trunk to China and in it I put . . ." naming a word that begins with the letter A—anteater, for example. The next player says, "I packed a trunk for China and in it I put an anteater and a baseball"—and so on. See if you can get all the way to Z. You can come up with other formats for this game. For example, if you're taking a long drive and everyone is getting hungry, you might play "I'm so hungry I could eat . . ." Name all the foods, in alphabetical order, that you're hungry enough to eat.

✎ **Listen to music together and try to learn the words to the songs.** The tune and the rhyme scheme will make it easier to memorize the words. If your child responds enthusiastically to lyrics, you might show her how to set other information to music.

✎ **Do a jigsaw puzzle together.** Clear a space on a card table or other surface where the family can work on the puzzle over several days. Working on the puzzle over time will improve your child's concentration and accustom her to working toward a long-range goal.

NINE

Fourth, Fifth, and Sixth Grades

B y the time your child enters fourth grade, he has firmly established his reading skills, he is using cursive writing, and he has a good grasp of his math facts. He is ready to take these basic skills and fly with them.

It's amazing to see what a reasonably motivated child in a reasonably strong school system can do in these three years. By the end of the sixth grade, your child will be able to carry on an intelligent conversation with you on a wide range of topics. He'll be able to read and understand many of the articles in your local newspaper. And his math skills may be considerably better than many adults'.

Ideally, his classroom is now a lively place where ideas are batted around and ambitious projects are conceived and executed. Reading plays a central role in all his studies and the teacher is able to impart information as well as skills.

Your child is also working hard at the important task of growing up. He is becoming increasingly independent, and investing more of his energies and emotional life at school, where he turns to teachers and friends for leadership and companionship. His comfort and happiness in the school environment will affect his willingness to apply himself academically.

How Language Arts Are Taught

Ideally, your child should experience a higher and more sophisticated quality of literature in the upper elementary grades than he did in the lower grades. He may still have a basal reading program, but the basal reader is more likely to be an anthology based on existing literature than a collection of entries written by educators. Even if the basal approach is still used, your child should be encouraged to visit the school library and select books on his own. Whatever the reading plan, the teacher will probably assign nonfiction as well as fiction.

While workbooks and worksheets continue to drill students in spelling and grammar information, there is a new emphasis on reading comprehension. As students start to read longer passages, teachers are concerned about whether students are really understanding what they read. It's one thing, after all, to be able to decipher all of the words in a given passage and another to really "get" what the passage is all about. Your child's teacher may begin directing him to look for the "clue" word or words that tell him what a passage is all about.

Teachers gauge reading comprehension in several ways. They may assign book reports or ask students to answer questions about the passages they've read. The questions may appear at the end of each section of the reader, or the teacher may pull questions from a teacher's manual or make up her own.

During these years, your child will be working on increasingly sophisticated writing assignments. A typical assignment might be to write a creative essay based on a single idea or first sentence the teacher supplies. (For example, your child might be asked to write an essay that begins with the sentence "I was walking home from school when the lights of the space ship first came into view.") He'll also have the chance to write compositions of his own choosing.

Increasingly, your child will be assigned expository writing, and will be asked to convey information rather than simply use his imagination. Your child may be asked to write book reports or to write about the things he's learned in school, especially in social studies.

How to Help with Reading

Your child should be reading well enough these days not to need any help from you. Even though he's reading on his own, chat with him about the books he's reading and make sure he knows you're interested. Here are some ways you can encourage your child to read beyond his class assignments:

✎ **Subscribe.** A great way to encourage reading is to let your child subscribe to a magazine. Send away for sample issues of several magazines and let your child choose which one he'd like to subscribe to. Here are some good candidates:

Boys' Life, Boy Scouts of America, 1325 West Walnut Hill Lane, Irving, TX 75015

Cricket, Box 51144, Boulder, CO 80321

Ranger Rick, National Wildlife Federation, 1400 16th Street, NW, Washington DC 20077

Kid City (from the publishers of *Sesame Street*), P.O. Box 51277, Boulder, CO 80321

Sports Illustrated for Kids, 500 Office Park Drive, Birmingham, AL 35223

3–2–1 Contact, E = MC Square, P.O. Box 51177, Boulder, CO 80321

Zillions, P.O. Box 51777, Boulder, CO 80321

✎ **Talk about the books or articles that *you're* reading.** If you're reading a murder mystery, for example, tell your child the plot as you go along and encourage him to help you figure out "whodunit." If you're reading a nonfiction book, tell him what interests you about this subject. Your child is old enough for a reasonably sophisticated discussion.

✎ **Start a series.** Did you have a favorite series of books when you were in elementary school? The Nancy Drew books were popular in the town where I grew up, and it was fun trading and sharing these books with my friends.

In fact, one of the reasons kids like series books is that they feed into children's urge to collect. Help your child to read all the books

Talking about Books

A great way to foster your child's interest in books is to talk with him about the books he reads. Here are some leading questions you might ask him:

- What's the book about? Who are the main characters and what do they do in the story?
- If you were making a movie of the book, which actors and actresses would you cast in the leading roles? Which parts would make good movie scenes?
- Who do you know who would really like this book?
- Did the book remind you of any other books you've read?

You may sometimes want to read the books your child is reading, both to get a sense of what interests him and so that you can have deeper discussions about his reading. Here are some conversation starters you can use if you've read the book:

- I really liked the part when————. What did you think about that part? What part did you like best?
- One part of the story confused me. Can you explain why ————?
- Reading the book made me want to know more about————.

in his favorite series. If you can afford to buy them (all of the books listed below are available in paperback), your child will enjoy displaying them on his bookshelf. If you take them out of the library, you might let him make a poster on which he can check off each book in the series as he reads it.

Series books don't always have the resonance or depth of classic children's literature but they can provide solid entertainment and good reading practice. Here are some of the better children's book series:

The Baby-Sitters Club by Ann M. Martin (Scholastic)
Encyclopedia Brown by Donald J. Sobol (Bantam)
Nancy Drew by Carolyn Keene (Archway)
The Hardy Boys by Franklin W. Dixon (Archway)

Mrs. Piggle-Wiggle by Betty MacDonald (Harper Trophy)
The Boxcar Children by Gertrude C. Warner (Albert Whitman)

Also, for sports enthusiasts, Matt Christopher's series of sports novels is a lot of fun. Titles (published by Little, Brown) include *Tough to Tackle* and *The Year Mom Won the Pennant.*

Note: Occasionally, children use book series in a way that is damaging. When reading a series of books becomes a craze or a fad in the classroom, students may brag about how many books in a given series they've read and tease and criticize classmates who haven't read as many. While it's fun to share and trade books, it isn't fun to be on the receiving end of a series-inspired put-down. So monitor your child's involvement and make sure he's reading for the right reasons.

✎ **When you're reading the newspaper, cut out articles that might interest your child.** He might enjoy a profile of a sports player or a TV personality he likes, as well as occasional news articles or even sections of advice columns, comics, and recipes.

How to Help Your Child with Book Reports

Despite their reputation as boring drudgery, book reports are really not such a bad idea. You can't argue with the main activity—reading a book—and the exercise of writing about a book can offer additional rewards.

The most important aspect of a book report is the book. If your child enjoys reading a book he'll relish the opportunity to share information about it. If reading the book was a chore, writing the report will be too. So make sure he has access to high quality, enjoyable books. Take a look at the books recommended on p. 116, talk to your children's librarian or a clerk in a children's bookstore, and make sure to respect your child's interests.

Ideally, your child's school will introduce book reports gradually. The first assignment may be to answer a series of questions about the book. As time goes on, the assignment may evolve into writing an essay about the book.

If your child hasn't been given this kind of gradual introduction to the world of book reports, you might suggest that he start thinking about ways of answering these questions:

1. Who was the main character in this book?
2. Did he or she tell the story, or was it told by a narrator?
3. What other characters were in the book?
4. How does the book begin?
5. What happens next?
6. Do the characters change at all over the course of the book?
7. How does the book end?
8. How did you feel when the book was over? Did it make you laugh or cry? Were you sorry it was over? Would you like to read it again?
9. What was the best part of the book?
10. What did you like least about this book?

How to Help with Reading Comprehension Homework

Sometime during the second half of elementary school, your child will begin to get reading comprehension assignments. He'll be asked to read a passage and then answer questions designed to test his understanding of what he's read. These kinds of comprehension questions crop up a lot on standardized tests, so it's important that your child learn how to do them.

In some ways, reading comprehension questions cut across the grain of what reading is all about. Some educators would argue that your child should be free to read a passage at his own speed and focus on the information that is most interesting to him. In practice however, reading is an important information-gathering tool, and children have to learn to absorb and retain facts that are presented in prose.

Here's how to help your child get the knack of doing reading comprehension exercises:

✎ **Show him how to isolate the main idea of the passage.** Just as he learned that subtraction is the reverse of addition, explain to your child that reading is the reverse of writing. He is learning how to write an effective essay by starting with a strong topic sentence and following with carefully ordered ideas. Ideally, the author of the passage he's reading has done the same thing. Often the first sentence will comprise the main idea in a nutshell. Other times, he'll have to look at the way the passage is organized and zero in on the main idea.

For example, take a look at the following paragraph:

The captain thought his troubles were over. But then his men staged a revolt. They met secretly and drew up a list of demands. If the demands weren't met, they said, they would not work.

Here the topic sentence is not the first one: "The captain thought his troubles were over." It's the second one: "But then his men staged a revolt." The topic sentence is followed by two supporting sentences, which expand upon and clarify the topic sentence.

✎ **Ask him to tell you about what he's read.** Sometimes the questions at the end of a passage can throw a child off. If he tells you about what he's read before answering the questions, your child may feel more confident.

✎ **Have him reread the passage.** If he still can't answer the questions, suggest that he read it again, possibly aloud. Of course, this will seem like a bore to him. He can make it more fun by reading as though he were a newscaster reporting on a late-breaking event or a gossipy old lady breathily imparting the newest town scandal.

✎ **Ask him to draw a picture.** This technique can be very helpful when the passage includes descriptive prose. For example, if your child has read a piece about how to build a house, he could draw a picture of a house, adding new elements as he reads about them.

How to Build Comprehension Skills

Here are some ways you can help your child develop the critical facility he needs to do reading comprehension exercises:

✎ **The Name Game.** When you go to a movie or read a book with your child, ask him what he thought of the story's title. Why does he think the author came up with that particular title? Can he think of a better one? Can he think of one that more accurately reflects the content of the story?

✎ **Tell me about it.** When your child reads a book or goes to a movie on his own, ask him to tell you all about it. Listen patiently— this is an excellent way for him to practice summarizing a story. (See the earlier box, "Talking about Books," for questions you can ask to get him talking.)

✎ **How was your day?** Some children come home brimming with information about what went on at school whereas others will answer the question "What happened today?" with an unconvincing "Nothing much." Even the kids who don't think they want to talk about their day are likely to start talking about particular incidents when you're all sitting around chatting. The dinner table is a wonderful place for people in the family to share information about what has happened to them during the day. If you share some stories about the things that happened to you that day, your child is likely to come up with stories about his day, too.

One parent finds out what happened during his daughter's day by asking specific questions. For example, he asks, "What was the *big* thing that happened today?" Sometimes it takes a while for his daughter to answer, but eventually she tells him what has been going on.

When your child tells you what happened, listen to everything he has to say. Though he doesn't know it, he is summarizing a series of events, just as he would in a book report. When he's finished, ask him questions that will help him reflect about the things that happened: "Why do you think the coach benched Jim and Frank?" "How did the fight between Karen and Melissa start?"

How to Help with Grammar Worksheets

In addition to the ongoing spelling studies, there will be a heavy emphasis during these years on learning correct grammar and punctuation. Many of the worksheets that come home during these years will concern proper use of periods, commas, semicolons, quotation marks, and so on. And your child will be learning about prefixes and suffixes, plurals, and other parts of speech.

You may have to do a little reviewing yourself if you're going to help your child with grammar worksheets. You might invest in a copy of a grammar book, such as *Essentials of English* by Vincent F. Hopper et al (Barrons).

Comedian Victor Borge does a routine in which he uses special sounds for each punctuation mark. You might try this out, talking to your child as usual but inserting appropriate sounds for commas, periods, colons, and so on. ("Oh *(squeak)* Sarah *(squeak)* dear *(squeak)* do you want Cheerios or toast for breakfast *(brrp)*") The results are pretty funny and a good lesson in punctuation. Your child will probably want to try this out as well.

How to Help Your Child with Writing Homework

Have you ever had to write an article or proposal? If writing isn't part of your daily work, you know how hard it can be to come up with an approach that will work and to find the words to express your ideas.

For some people it is harder to create a piece of personal writing than to write more objective prose. Picture yourself sitting down to write a letter to an old friend whom you haven't seen for a long time. Where do you begin? What can you say to your friend that will give her an image of where you are now in your life?

Thinking about how hard writing can be should make it easier to sympathize with your child when he complains about a tough writing assignment. Fortunately, there are strategies that can help anyone burst through writer's block, freeing young writers (and even older ones!) to get to work. Here they are:

✎ **Brainstorm.** Before he writes the first sentence of his essay, your child should take the time to think about what he wants to write. The best way for him to do this is to allow himself a period of time to throw out ideas and let random associations lead him to his creation.

Let's say you live in New York and your child has been given an assignment to write an essay about life in New York City. Tell your child to take a blank piece of paper and jot down any ideas that come to him. During the brainstorming phase your child can draw or doodle on the page as well as write down words and sentence fragments.

When you're teaching your child to brainstorm, do it with him a few times. The first time, for example, you could act as his secretary and write down ideas as they come to him. Ask him questions like: "What do you like about living in New York?" "What are the bad things about New York?" "How does living in New York compare to living in other places you've visited?" Eventually he'll be able to complete this process on his own.

✎ **Focus.** Now that your child has tapped into his creativity, ideas should come more easily. Have him look over the words he's written down and think about what he'd like to write about. He may want to circle the fragments that especially interest him. He needn't cross out the bits that seem irrelevant—they may come back into the story later on.

✎ **Organize.** So now your child is ready to write, right? Wrong. Right now a lot of ideas are tumbling around in his brain, and that's great. But if he just starts writing them out, he's more than likely to put the cart before the horse. The result may be full of promise and creativity, but he probably won't have the maturity it requires to rewrite a jumbled mess into a coherent essay. He needs to keep himself on track by organizing his ideas. There are several ways he can do that, including these:

- Clustering. Show him how to take his random ideas and cluster them into groups of related ideas. He can draw circles around the related words.
- Outlining. When he is older, your child will probably learn how to create an elaborate outline. For now, it is enough for him to write down a sequence of ideas. Encourage him to create an introductory and concluding paragraph, using the ideas he has jotted down. Your child's outline for an essay about his life in New York might look something like this:

Living in New York is different: apartment not house; hallways not backyard; travel by bus, subway, taxi, walking, not car.

Good things for kids to do: Central Park (zoo, bikes, rowboats, playground, puppet shows); Natural History Museum; Empire State Building; World Trade Center.

Problems with New York: danger (muggings, robberies); homelessness; dirt and pollution; AIDS.

New York is special because: movies; Broadway shows; music; United Nations; Lincoln Center.

I like New York because: friends; family; school; it's fun and exciting.

- Story mapping. If your child is a visual person, he may prefer working from a story map. A story map is a graphic representation of the essay he plans to write. Put each main idea inside a circle or rectangle. Supporting arguments can radiate from each main idea. Use lines to connect the ideas.
- Indexing. A fourth approach is to use index cards to organize your child's essay. Let him put each of his ideas on an index card. Now he can shuffle and arrange his index cards so that they follow a natural progression. Show him how to use other index cards (possibly of a different color) to write down the main idea of each paragraph. He can work from the cards to write his essay, or he might actually write a single sentence on each card. Then he can edit the sentences on the cards.

  The index card method can be particularly useful if your child is writing a research project. During the note-taking phase (see pp. 175–176), your child might record nuggets of information on index cards, being careful to note the source of the information on each card. Then he can shuffle these cards along with cards on which he records his own ideas and thoughts to create an overall plan.
- Create topic sentences. The topic sentence approach to writing doesn't always yield the most creative essays. But it is a good way to keep an essay organized and coherent. Show your child how to come up with a topic sentence that clearly introduces the theme of each paragraph. (He should have learned about topic sentences and supporting sentences while doing his reading comprehension homework—see pp. 150–151.)

One way to think about topic sentences is to regard them as the answers to questions. For example, your child might ask himself the question "What are the bad things about living in New York?" And he might answer something like this: "New York has many problems, including crime, dirt, and pollution." This topic sentence could be followed up (later in the writing process) by supporting sentences, like: "It's dangerous to walk in certain neighborhoods in New York or to go out late at night. A friend of mine's father was mugged once. And once our TV was stolen. Garbage piles up on the streets and it smells bad in the summer." And so on.

✎ **Draft.** Working from his story map, outline, or topic sentences (or a combination), your child can now begin writing. Since he'll write a draft first, he should feel free to let his ideas flow, without getting too concerned about the niceties of spelling and punctuation. If he gets stuck, he should look back over his brainstorming notes, to remember his original ideas.

✎ **Read.** Now your child should read over what he's written. It's a very good idea to read out loud, because by hearing his prose your child will have a chance to judge what "sounds" right and what needs changing.

✎ **Edit.** Now it's time for the finishing touches that will make his essay really great. Tell your child to go back over his essay and make changes. In some ways, this is the most important part of the process, the part that makes the difference between a mediocre paper and a really good one. It's best if your child can leave his draft overnight before embarking on the edit. Have him go over the paper line by line, changing words, correcting spelling, punctuation, and grammar, and clarifying his ideas. You may or may not want to go over the paper with him, pointing out problems. If you do, make sure you don't take over the writing of the piece. Your job is to help him improve upon *his* paper, not to write a new one for him.

✎ **Rewrite.** Now all he has to do is create a clean copy of his edited draft. Make sure he allots enough time and has the materials he needs.

Help for Poor Spellers

No matter how carefully he studies his weekly spelling list, your child may just be a poor speller. Learning disabilities can cause poor spelling (see pp. 193–196), but even children who are not so afflicted can have a lot of trouble spelling accurately.

Unfortunately, poor spelling on essays and other papers makes the author look careless. If your child is a poor speller, he needs some way of compensating. Here are some tools that will help.

✎ **Personal spelling file.** If your child consistently misspells certain words, it may help for him to start his own spelling dictionary. A small address book, with tabs for each letter of the alphabet, will work

A Friendly Game of Ghost

Ghost is great fun for a long car ride, and it's good spelling practice too. The first player says a letter—let's say *E*. The next player adds a letter to the first player's letter—let's say *IE*. You can add letters either before or after the other letters. The game continues until someone forms a word or else is unable to think of a word that includes those letters. If a player can't think of a word, he or she can try to fake. If you fake, the next player can challenge you, and if you can't come up with a real word that includes those letters, you lose the round. If you can come up with a word, the person who challenged you loses the round. When you lose a round, you get a letter, starting with *G*. The first person to get all five letters, *GHOST,* loses.

Here is an example to show you how the game is played. Let's say someone has spelled *RIEND*. The next player doesn't want to add an *F* to form *FRIEND* so he adds an *S* to form *RIENDS*. Is the next player stuck spelling *FRIENDS*? No—she adds an *H: RIENDSH*. The next player challenges her. But the first player has a word in mind: *FRIENDSHIP*. So the challenger gets a letter.

Using the Dictionary

A dictionary is an invaluable addition to your child's reference library. But you can't just give him a dictionary and assume he'll know how to use it, or that his teacher will have given a lesson in dictionary usage. Show him how the dictionary is arranged in alphabetical order. Following each entry, the word is spelled phonetically, so that you can find out how it's pronounced. Look at the key to find out how to decode phonetic spellings. Usually the dictionary gives more than one definition, in order of importance.

"Dictionary" is a fun game that reinforces dictionary skills. It's best played with four or more people. One person takes the dictionary and looks for a word none of the others has ever heard of. Each of the other players writes down an imaginary definition of the word. Everyone hands his definition to the first player, who now reads aloud each definition, including the dictionary's. Everyone guesses which definition is correct.

nicely. Have him write the correct spelling of his most commonly misspelled words on the appropriate pages.

✎ **A special dictionary.** Get your child a copy of *How to Spell It: A Dictionary of Commonly Misspelled Words* by Harriet Wittles and Joan Greisman (Grosset and Dunlap). Here your child can look up the word the way he spells it and find the correct spelling.

✎ **Computerized spell check.** If you have a computer, consider letting your child use it to write his essays. Most word processing programs come with an automatic spell check. The spell check will stop at each misspelled word and display an array of alternatives. By selecting the correct word, your child may learn how to spell it.

✎ **Extra care.** Help your child to understand that spelling matters to teachers, bosses, and other people in authority. Although it's a drag to take the extra time, your child should go over his papers carefully and look up any words that he's not sure of.

How to Encourage Writing

Even though school forces your child to write about a certain number of prescribed topics, your child should also have abundant opportunities to write for sheer pleasure. Here are some ways you can help build your child's writing skills:

✎ **Dear Diary.** Your child is at an age when keeping a journal may be very appealing. Buy him a diary with a lock, or a cloth-covered notebook. Be sure to respect his privacy if he wants to keep his journal secret.

✎ **Dear Mr. President.** Encourage your child to write to local and national politicians about issues that concern him. In most cases, he should get at least a form letter back, and may well get onto the politician's mailing list.

✎ **Fan mail.** Your child may also want to write a fan letter to his favorite writer, performer, or sports player. Again, the person's office will probably respond with a form letter and possibly a picture. Make sure your child understands that he will probably not receive a personal reply to his mail.

Language Arts Games

Clue

Scrabble

Scattergories Junior

Language Arts Software

Grammar Examiner (Design Ware/Britannica Software)

Grammar Gremlins (Davidson)

How Math Is Taught

By now your child should be familiar with the four basic math concepts—addition, subtraction, multiplication, and division. During the second half of elementary school, he will learn to perform increasingly complex operations involving these concepts. He'll also learn about fractions, percentages, decimals, and graphs. Toward the end of elementary school, he'll start learning basic geometry and algebra.

By the time he leaves sixth grade, your child may begin to work with positive and negative numbers. He may also be exposed to the concept of prime numbers. He'll be learning some rudimentary algebra and geometry. He'll need to be comfortable identifying and writing numbers up to 1,000,000,000. He'll be able to apply the four basic mathematical operations to money and other decimal equations, and he'll be able to manipulate fractions even when they have different denominators.

Unavoidably, math involves drill. Night after night, worksheets full of problems will come home, and your child will have to labor over solving them. Some worksheets are better written than others, however. Creative publishers inject variety into the problems, tie them to real-life situations, liven them up with pictures and cartoons, and provide some progression so that children learn as they work.

Some children who have trouble reading nevertheless flourish at math. Your child may have an easier time understanding math symbols and relating them to concrete reality than he has with words.

How to Help with Math Homework

In order to begin the complex computations that are taught in the upper elementary grades, your child needs a firm grasp of the number concepts that were taught in the lower grades. If for some reason these concepts have been a problem all along, it will be well worth your while to work with your child—or hire a tutor—to help explain basic math concepts. The summer before he starts fourth grade would be a good time for your child to work on these math facts. (See pages 63–68.)

If you find you need to go back and review math facts, remember to use "manipulatives"—like buttons or pennies or blocks—to convey concepts. It's not enough to memorize the multiplication tables if you don't understand what they mean.

If your child needs help with his math homework, try to be as upbeat, positive, and encouraging as possible. It can be really frustrating to stand over a child who just can't "get" a problem that seems so simple to you. Remember that math comprehension is a progressive, developmental skill. Praise your child lavishly for the problems (or parts of problems) he gets right and offer positive encouragement for solving tough ones.

In many cases, your child will be learning a different approach to tackling math problems from the one you were taught. Don't confuse him by trying to teach him your way. If you can't understand the way he's being taught and are unable to help him, arrange a conference with his teacher. She should be happy to sit down with you and explain the concepts so that you can help your child.

Here are some ways you can help with a variety of math problems:

Complex Computations

In order to perform complex multiplication computations, your child needs to have mastered his multiplication math facts. Trying to count 7×8 on his fingers while multiplying 508×74 is sure to get him into trouble. So review these math facts if you need to. Here's how to help with complex computations.

✎ **Multiplication.** Just as with addition and subtraction, getting the right answer in multiplication depends on lining up the numbers correctly. Again, graph paper can be very helpful. One of the hardest things for most kids to learn is how to handle zeros in either part of the equation. Find out how your school has taught your child to handle these situations and make sure he understands the rules.

✎ **Division.** Long division is usually the last of the basic math operations to be taught and is generally considered the hardest. As with other math operations, precision and neatness make a big difference. Have your child work on graph paper and make sure that as he works he puts the numbers in the correct columns. It may help to circle the part of the division problem that he is working on at any moment.

"**M**y son has had a hard time in math, ever since he started sixth grade. When he started, he didn't grasp decimals or fractions, so we had to sit down with him and explain the concepts. We had a lot of difficulty because we'd try to explain it one way and he would say, 'But that's not the way the teacher does it.'

"Another problem was the math textbook. There aren't enough examples and the explanation is very brief and never goes into enough depth about how to arrive at the answers. It's been very confusing and frustrating for all of us. Instead of using the math problems as extra examples, we've made up our own extra examples which we work through with him. We try to use daily things. Like, we'll say, "If you have so many Mike Schmidt baseball cards and you have so many Dave Stewarts . . ." Then we'll actually use his baseball cards—if he can see it in front of him, he does much better.

"Working with him, we've helped him improve his math grades. Still, I believe we'll have to continue to help him."

—Lou Ann S.

Decimals

Decimals can be really confusing when a child first learns about them. One of the best ways to help your child understand decimals is to use money as an example. A quarter is actually $.25. Two dimes equal $.2 (or $.20). A penny is a hundredth of a dollar, or $.01. Now compare a penny, a dime, a dollar, ten dollars, and a hundred dollars: $.01, $.10, $1.00, $10.00, $100.00. Try adding $100 + 25 cents. How would you do it? What if there were a monetary system in which there were 1000 pennies to a dollar? Then you could have an amount like $77.999. Use graph paper and have your child use a separate square for the decimal point. Remind him to line up the decimal points in addition and subtraction problems. When your child begins multiplying and dividing decimals, make sure you know the rules governing these procedures so you can help as needed.

Fractions

Fractions can be daunting, especially if your child doesn't catch on when they are first presented. You can help by bringing the abstract symbols back down to the concrete. When your child is first learning fractions, show him how easy it is to divide something into fractional parts. Cut his sandwich into five equal pieces and ask him to hand you two fifths. Put a stack of quarters in front of him and ask him to divide the stack in half. How many quarters are there in each half?

Even when fractions become more complex, you can still use concrete objects to help your child understand his homework. Use orange slices, settings of silverware, or other dividable items to give concrete examples. For example, suppose your child has to add ¾ + ½. Take two apples and cut one in quarters, the other in half. Show your child that by adding three of the four quarters to one half-apple you get a whole apple, with one quarter left over. The answer: 1¼. Now convert the problem into a mathematical equation. To do that you need to convert the ½ apple into quarters by cutting it in half. Now you have 5/4 apple, or 1¼ apples.

Percentages

Percentages are generally easier to understand than fractions, since they are based on a hundred and since the base doesn't change. Some children are confused by the fact that a percentage can be either more or less than 1. For example, 300% = 3, 3% = 3/100. If your child has a firm grasp of fractions, you can ask him to see percentages in terms of hundredths. Another approach is to compare percentages to money. 25% of a dollar is 25 cents. 125% of a dollar is $1.25.

Graphs

As the word suggests, a graph is a graphic way of expressing mathematical information. In the upper elementary grades, your child is likely to encounter three kinds of graph: circle graphs, bar graphs, and line graphs. Like other mathematical concepts, graphs appeal more to

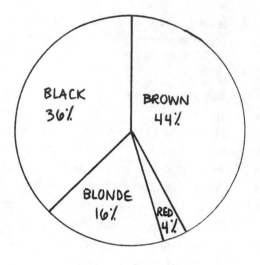

HAIR COLOR IN ROOM 404

some people than others. If your child finds graphs baffling, point out that a graph is a way of looking at a lot of information at once. Instead of having to read "45% preferred chocolate, 30% preferred vanilla, and 25% were undecided," you can look at a graph and see at once who preferred what, which was most popular, and so on.

✎ **Circle graphs.** The circle graph is the easiest to understand. Encourage your child to think of this graph as a pie, with various-sized slices given to various eaters.

✎ **Bar graphs.** It's a little harder to make out "at a glance" what a bar graph is all about. The key is to understand that this graph must be read carefully. Read the title of the graph and then the information going down the side and across the bottom. What do the marks along the side and bottom measure? What is this graph all about? Encourage your child to spend time studying the graph before he leaps in and tries to answer any questions about it.

✎ **Line graphs.** A line graph usually charts progress, or change over time: a company's sales, pages of a book read in a single night, and so on. It can have the same structure as a bar graph, with information down the side and across the bottom, but instead of being

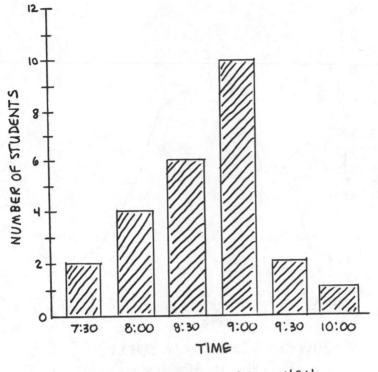

BEDTIMES IN ROOM 404

plotted with thick bars, the information is plotted in points, with a line connecting the points to show change over time.

Your child may be asked to create a graph, either as part of his math homework or as part of a science or social studies research project. If so, ask him to think about what kind of information he could show in a graph and what kind of graph would best show that information. Usually, a circle graph is best for illustrating percentages. (If you did a study of people's breakfast choices, for example, you could use a circle graph to show the percentage of people who chose each item.) A bar graph is a good choice if you want to show two variables—quantity and time, for example. (If you wanted to show how many people arrived in class on time for each day of the week, for example, you might use a bar graph.) When you want to show a progression, a line graph is probably your best choice. (For example, if your child wanted to show his progress swimming laps, he could use

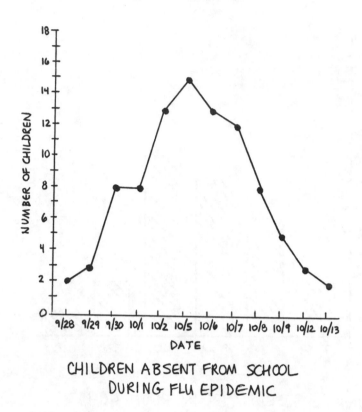

CHILDREN ABSENT FROM SCHOOL
DURING FLU EPIDEMIC

a line graph to chart how many laps he could swim over a period of time.)

Number Recognition

By the time he left third grade, your child was probably identifying numbers up to 10,000. In the second half of elementary school, your child will learn to read and write numbers up to 1,000,000,000. Number recognition can be difficult, especially when your child sees a number like 1005, which looks suspiciously like one hundred and five.

Take a sheet of graph paper and go over thirteen of the vertical lines with a pencil. Now show your child how to fill in a one-digit number using the far right column, a two-digit number using the two far right columns and so on until you reach 1,000,000,000. Have him say each number aloud.

Now show your child how to insert commas and teach him that the comma is the place where you say billion, million, or thousand.

(Numbers between 1000 and 9999 are often written without a comma, while 10,000 and up contain the comma. Explain to your child that this is just one of those annoying exceptions—the kind that happen all the time in writing and almost never in math.)

Story Problems

Sometime during this second half of elementary school, your child will begin to work with "story problems" (or "word problems"). You probably remember story problems; they go something like this: "John invited four of his friends home from school with him for a snack. There were only three apples. How could he divide the apples so that everyone had an equal amount?" In this case the task is to divide the three apples among the five children. The equation is: 3 [apples] ÷ (4 + 1) [children] = 3/5 [apple per child].

Some children respond readily to this kind of problem while others find story problems baffling. How on earth can your child turn this story into a math problem? And who cares about John and his stupid apples anyway? Even if your child figures out how to go about working the problem, one little detail can mess up the whole problem. In this story problem, for example, it's easy to read the phrase

Neatness Counts

Math is a science. There can be an infinite number of answers to the question "What did you do for your summer vacation?" but only one answer to the question "What is 9 + 5?"

The more complex the math problem, the more opportunities there are to make a small error that yields the wrong answer. Sloppiness—scribbling the numbers, misaligning a column of numbers, and so on—is a sure-fire way to get a wrong answer.

Even if your child is not naturally neat, he needs to learn how to be neat when working math problems. Urge him to take his time and do the work carefully. If he complains that this makes the homework take too long, point out that it will get done sooner if he gets the answers right the first time.

"four of his friends" and assume that four is the number into which the apple should be divided, instead of adding in John to make five children.

The key to helping your child with this kind of problem is helping him understand that there is really nothing mysterious or abstract about this situation. Ask him to visualize John and his friends. Have him think about the three apples and how they need to be divided among the children. You could even take out three apples and set five places at your kitchen table. The more plausible this story becomes, the more likely your child is to "get" it.

If your child likes to draw, you might encourage him to make a picture of the events that take place in a story problem. When he can visualize the situation, he'll have an easier time arriving at the right equation.

Another approach is to ask your child to underline the important information in each story problem. In this case, the key information is: *John, four friends, three apples.* By underlining this information, he breaks the story into its component parts. Once your child has identified the key information, he should think about a strategy: what kind of mathematical equation is needed for this problem?

If your child isn't a strong reader, story problems may be made extra hard by his confusion about how to read them. Since a story problem is not a reading assignment, it should be all right with your child's teacher if you read the problem aloud to him.

How to Reinforce Math Skills

As your child moves through the upper grades, continue to make math part of his everyday life. Here are some ideas:

✎ **Talk about shapes.** When you make a sandwich for a child, point out that the sandwich is a square. What happens if you cut it in half down the middle? What if you cut it in half diagonally? What if you cut it in quarters? Point out the different shapes of street signs— the triangular yield sign, the hexagonal stop sign, and so on.

✎ **Sports provide a great opportunity to talk about math.** No die-hard baseball fan can say that math is useless when it helps him understand how to calculate earned run averages or runs batted in. If your child follows the Olympics, he'll need a facility with decimals to understand the judges' scoring.

✎ **Check, please.** In a restaurant, ask your child to add up the check to make sure it's right. He may even want to get the menu out and make sure the server listed the correct prices.

✎ **Speedy solutions.** When you're driving, call your child's attention to the speedometer. If you have fifty miles to go and you're driving 40 miles an hour, how soon can you expect to get there? Show him how the odometer works, too. Let's say you're driving to Grandma's and you have five miles to go. Because of traffic, your speed varies—45 miles an hour on smooth stretches, 25–40 when the road is more crowded. About how long will it take to get there? You could also talk about gas mileage. If your car's gas tank holds so many gallons and goes so many miles before it needs refueling, how many miles does it get to the gallon?

✎ **Crafty answers.** Many crafts call on math skills. If your child is interested in woodworking, for example, he'll have to learn to estimate, measure, and use other math operations with precision. If he enjoys pottery, he might become involved in mixing and measuring glazes.

✎ **Get an outdoor thermometer.** Choose one that shows both Fahrenheit and Celsius temperatures. The Celsius thermometer (and on rare occasions the Fahrenheit as well) will help him understand negative numbers as he perceives the meaning of "5 below zero." And comparing the two temperatures will help him to understand how different number systems work.

✎ **Practice estimation.** Estimation is a vitally important math tool, so find opportunities to estimate in everyday life. Let's say you're grocery shopping with your child. You only have $50 with you, so you have to make sure your bill comes to less than that. Unless you bring along a calculator (which you may want to try sometime, too), it's too complicated to add up each item to the penny. Show your child how to round off each item to the nearest dollar and keep a running total as you add each item.

✎ **Read up on math.** Your child will have fun with *Sideways Arithmetic from the Wayside School* by Louis Sachar (Scholastic).

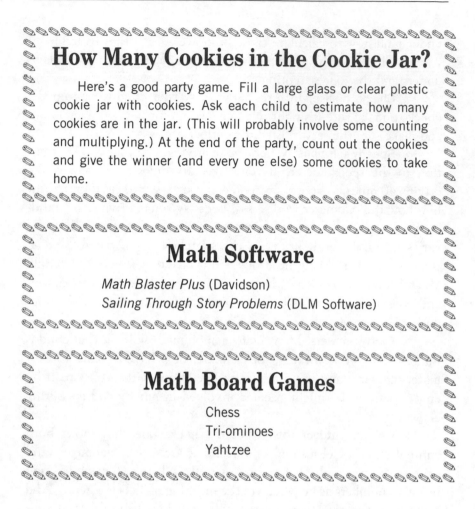

How Many Cookies in the Cookie Jar?

Here's a good party game. Fill a large glass or clear plastic cookie jar with cookies. Ask each child to estimate how many cookies are in the jar. (This will probably involve some counting and multiplying.) At the end of the party, count out the cookies and give the winner (and every one else) some cookies to take home.

Math Software

Math Blaster Plus (Davidson)
Sailing Through Story Problems (DLM Software)

Math Board Games

Chess
Tri-ominoes
Yahtzee

How Social Studies Is Taught

Now that your child is in the upper elementary grades, he probably has a social studies textbook. He'll probably start off by learning about his state, and then, through grades five and six, about the nation and the world. As he studies an ever-expanding terrain, he'll spend more time looking at maps and atlases and gaining a sense of the world's dimensions. A good deal of his homework will consist of reading passages in this textbook and absorbing the information so that he can be tested on it.

One major problem with this process is that many social studies

textbooks are tedious, if not downright boring. In the course of researching this book, I spent many long hours in the stacks of the
Teachers College Library at Columbia University, poring over textbooks. Sitting on the floor of an airless, dusty room, staring at textbooks, I found my eyes glazing over and my mind turning numb. I had
to stretch and walk around to stay awake. The very format of these
books, with their thick, heavy covers, monotonous columns of text,
and uninspiring illustrations, is enough to turn anyone off.

Creative teachers supplement the textbook with entertaining historical novels, other additional reading, and hands-on experiences.
When your child is studying the American settlement of the Midwest,
for example, the teacher might assign the book *The Courage of Sarah
Noble,* by Alice Dalgliesh, which is about a pioneer girl. Or she might
assign or read aloud to the class passages from Laura Ingalls Wilder's
Little House series. She might organize a project in which the class
prepares and eats a typical pioneer meal or uses scraps of old fabric to
sew a patchwork quilt.

How much your child enjoys social studies depends to a large
extent on the quality of his textbook and his teacher's ingenuity and
energy. There is much that you can do at home, though, to make
social studies—and social studies homework—more interesting.

How to Help with Social Studies Homework

If you are familiar with the material your child is studying, you can
help by initiating casual dinner-table conversations on the subject. If
you happen to know something about immigration, for example, and
your child is studying how Europeans came to America in the nineteenth century, you could talk to him about the famines, political
persecution, and personal ambitions that led many Europeans to come
to America. If your own ancestors came to America from Europe, you
could share anecdotes about their experiences. If your ancestors came
to America from other parts of the world, you could tell your child
about their experiences in the context of whatever your child is
learning.

At this stage, a good deal of social studies homework takes the form of reading comprehension homework. Your child will probably be asked to read a passage in the textbook or workbook and then answer questions based on his reading.

If your child is given reading assignments in his textbook, show him how to read in a way that prepares him for classroom tests. Before he begins reading a chapter in his textbook, he should survey the chapter by reading and thinking about its title, reading any subtitles, and looking at the illustrations and their captions.

If there are questions at the end of the chapter, it may be a good idea for your child to take a look at them *before* he starts reading the chapter. This way he can be aware of the central points the book expects him to grasp. (Make sure he reads the whole chapter word for word, even though he knows what the questions are.)

How to Help Your Child Read Maps

Geography is no longer a discrete subject in most American elementary schools, but your child is likely to work with maps in the course of his social studies homework. We adults are used to maps, so it may come as a surprise if your child is completely baffled by the maps he encounters. Sit down with him and show him how maps are made. You might use a map of your town as an introduction, because your child will recognize familiar landmarks and will be able to relate reality to the images on the map.

Here are some activities that will help him become more comfortable with maps:

✎ **Help your child get in tune with your immediate neighborhood.** Take a walk around the block and point out landmarks. When you leave the house, which way do you turn to go to the shopping center? Which way to school? Show your child how to make a map of your immediate neighborhood.

✎ **Make him your navigator.** When you're driving somewhere, give your child the map and show him the route you plan to take. Then you can ask him to navigate.

✎ **Map your team.** If your child follows sports, look at the map whenever his team is playing an away game. Point out where the games are being played.

How to Help Your Child Handle a Research Project

"The bane of my existence" is how one parent described research projects to me. It's true that when you're already busy working, raising a family, and keeping the household running smoothly the last thing you may want to hear is that your child has a major research project due at the end of next week.

Nevertheless, unlike more questionable activities, learning to research is time well spent. If you can help your child become an effective researcher, you'll give him a tool that will be invaluable throughout his educational career and indeed throughout his life. Research is the cornerstone of many educational disciplines, but all too frequently students arrive in college with very limited research skills.

In a first-rate school, your child will be taught everything he needs to know about doing a research project before he gets his first assignment. Unfortunately, given time constraints and other burdens, your child's teacher may have sent him home ill-prepared for this kind of work. If so, you'll have to help. Here's how:

✎ **Make a time plan.** As I discussed in Chapter 3, the biggest problem you can have with a research project is trying to do it all at the last minute. As soon as your child gets the assignment, you should sit down together with a calendar and plan how he's going to complete it. Depending on what the project is, you'll probably want to break it into stages. Here are some fairly typical steps:

1. *Do preliminary research.* Let's say the project is open-ended—"write a biographical study of a famous American." Your child will need to do some preliminary research before he can focus on his exact topic. Perhaps he has a book that will help him decide. Or he may need to go to the library.

2. *Decide on a topic.* In the case of the preceding assignment, this means picking an individual to write about. It's your child's job, not yours, to pick the topic, so avoid making too many suggestions. Perhaps the librarian can give him some ideas, or maybe he'll get one from browsing through books and exhibits. Make sure, considering the preliminary research, that there is enough information available for an entire research project.

3. *Purchase supplies.* If the project calls for a visual component like a chart or model, make sure you gather a list of supplies early on. Purchase the supplies well before your child will need them. Buy plenty—there may be a few mistakes along the way.

4. *Research.* This may mean going to the library, visiting a museum, or interviewing people. Taking notes is part of the research process.

5. *Write.* Writing includes all the stages described earlier: brainstorming, outlining, drafting, editing, and rewriting. When you make your schedule, aim to have the project completed a few days ahead of its due date. That way you'll have some leeway if you fall behind.

✎ **Organize the material.** Ideally, when the research is done, your child will have more information than he needs to write his paper. His task now is to sift through the material he has, selecting what he needs and organizing it into a coherent outline. In some ways a research paper is easier to write than a creative writing assignment. Here it's not so much a question of imagination as of simple organization. Show your child how to use the organizing techniques described on p. 154 to bring his material together. He might jot down some key words from each part of his research and use them as he would in a brainstorming session. Ask him to think about which ideas belong together and to group related ideas into sections or paragraphs.

✎ **Start writing!** Have your child use the writing techniques described on pp. 153–156.

✎ **Or start building!** Don't assume that a visual project will take less time than a written one. In fact, the visual project may take longer, especially if your child hits snags along the way. Just as a written project goes through stages, so does a visual one. Your child should start with a sketch of his project and a complete list of the information and supplies he'll need. He should plan each component of the project. Make sure he gets to work well in advance of the deadline so he has time to correct mistakes.

Teach Your Child How to Take Notes

Once you've identified the research materials your child needs to use, teach him how to take notes. Notetaking is a fine art that takes time to learn. One way to help your child understand what he needs to do is to have him jot down some questions before he begins researching. When did the person he's studying live and die? Where did she grow up? What did she do that made her famous? How did she affect the world around her? What special talents or skills did she have? What problems or challenges did she face? As he researches, your child can look for answers to these questions.

There are different ways to take notes, depending on the source you're using. Here are some suggestions:

✎ **Books.** The key to note taking from books is not to record word for word the things we read there but rather to know how to summarize them. At first, your child might try writing a single sentence for each paragraph or page that he reads. He should also start to learn how to read only those passages that are relevant to his assignment. For example, if the library has five or six long biographies of the person he is writing about, he won't be expected to read every word of all those books. He should look them over to see which ones are written in a style he's comfortable with and which ones have the information he needs. When he has identified the passages he needs to know about, he should read those sections carefully. If your child owns the book he is working with, you may want to let him use a special highlighting pen to emphasize key passages.

✎ **Museums and historical buildings.** At a museum or a historical building (such as the State House or the home of a historical figure), your child has quite a different task. Rather than summarize someone else's writing, he has to write down his own information based on his impressions. Encourage him to think about the questions he formulated before he arrived and to write down his answers. He should also write down his impressions. Instead of writing every minute, he should look at the relevant artifacts—perhaps at an entire room— and then jot down the information he needs. Make sure your child takes home any pamphlets, brochures, or other literature that will help him with correct spelling of names and other information.

✎ **Interviewing people.** The advantage of interviewing a real live person is that your child can get answers to his specific questions. The disadvantage is that the person may ramble on with a lot of seemingly irrelevant responses. Your child will have to try to redirect the conversation without appearing rude. Although you would discourage your child from writing down the content of a book word for word, he may want to quote directly from the people he interviews. The best approach may be to tape-record the interview. Then he can listen to his recording at home and make notes, including verbatim quotes of some material.

Note taking is easier and more fun when you use abbreviations. If your child is researching Jane Addams, for example, he can use the initials J. A. He can also use the + sign for "and" and abbreviations like "v." for "very," "wld." for "would," and so on. Just make sure he doesn't overdo it so he forgets what his abbreviations stand for! He may also want to take his notes on index cards. He can write one nugget of information on each card. Then he can arrange his cards into an outline for the project.

How to Encourage Social Studies

Here are some ways you can ensure that your child's understanding of social studies extends beyond the material he learns in class.

✎ **Take a field trip.** Is there a historical restoration in your area, or a museum with artifacts from another culture? If so, by all means visit. A visit to your state capital or, if possible, to Washington, D.C., will be fun and informative. Look for ways of learning about other cultures. Does your child like Chinese food? Stop and talk about what makes Chinese food different from American food. Why do the Chinese use more rice and less meat than Americans do? If he's

Social Studies Reading

Biographies—good ones, that is—are a wonderfully painless way to learn about history. Historical novels can also teach children about the past. Ask your children's librarian for suggestions. Here are some possibilities:

Lost Star: The Story of Amelia Earhart by Patricia Lauber (Scholastic)

Martin Luther King, Jr. by Robert Jakoubek (Chelsea House)

Jump Ship to Freedom, War Comes to Willy Freeman, and *Who Is Carrie* by James L. Collier and Christopher Collier (Delacorte) —black experience during the Revolutionary War

Sing Down the Moon by Scott O' Dell (Dell)—the Navajo Indians' "Long March"

Number the Stars by Lois Lowry (Dell)—two Danish girls in World War II

Harriet Tubman, Conductor on the Underground Railroad by Ann Petry (Archway)

Little House on the Prairie and other Little House books by Laura Ingalls Wilder (Harper)—American frontier

In the Year of the Boar and Jackie Robinson by Bette Bao Lord (Harper)—immigration, 1940s

Dragonwings by Laurence Yep (Harper)—Chinese immigrants in San Francisco, 1900s

Escape from Warsaw by Ian Serraillier (Scholastic)—World War II Europe

Across Five Aprils by Irene Hunt (Berkley)—Civil War

Sarah Bishop by Scott O'Dell (Scholastic)—Revolutionary War

Tituba of Salem Village by Ann Petry (Harper Trophy)—Salem witch trials

interested in martial arts, find out how various self-defense techniques are a part of Japanese or Chinese culture.

✎ **Play the license plate game.** When you're on vacation, encourage your child to look for license plates from different states.

Social Studies Games

Risk
State to State

Social Studies Software

Where in the World Is Carmen Sandiego (Broderbund)
Also in this series: *Where in the USA Is Carmen Sandiego,*
Where in Europe Is Carmen Sandiego, and *Where in Time Is Carmen Sandiego.*

Before you go, make a large chart with the names of all fifty states. Let each person in the family make a guess as to how many different states you'll see, or which license plates you'll see most often. Have your child put a check next to the name of the state every time he sees that state's plate. (This is a good lesson in geography as well. You're more likely to see an Oklahoma license plate when you're driving through Texas than when you're driving through Connecticut. Your child will begin to take an interest in the location of the various states when that information is relevant to the game he's playing.)

✎ **Talk about current events.** Newspapers abound with stories of interest to children this age. For example, when the Atlanta Braves met the Minnesota Twins for the 1991 World Series, Native American groups staged a protest. They felt that the Braves' fans' use of war paint, chanting, and tomahawk wielding was racist and perpetuated stereotypes about Native Americans. The fans claimed their cheering technique showed respect for the Native Americans. This is the kind of story that is likely to interest your child, especially if he's been studying Native Americans in school.

✎ **Dear pen pal.** Encourage your child to become a pen pal with someone in another country. Two organizations that can help are:

Student Letter Exchange
630 Third Avenue
New York, NY 10017

Gifted Children's Pen Pals International
c/o Dr. Debby Sue Van de Vender
166 East 61st Street
New York, NY 10021

✎ **Talk about your family's history.** From which countries did your child's ancestors come to America? Take books about these countries out of the library and read them together. Why did your ancestors leave their native countries? What was it like when they got here? How have things changed? Encourage your own parents to talk to your child about their childhoods. Ask them to share the family photo album with your child. If he's interested, encourage him to tape-record an oral history of your parents' and other family members' recollections.

How Science Is Taught

As in the lower elementary school grades, science education can be as dull or fascinating, as sketchy or rich, as the program your school offers.

In addition to the topics that you remember under the heading *science* from your own elementary school days, a number of new subjects may be included in your child's science education. Human sexuality, drugs, and AIDS may all be topics in your child's science curriculum.

While there is general agreement (with a good deal of individual variation) on the kinds of things children should study in language arts and math and even to a lesser degree in social studies, there is no accepted national curriculum governing science. Essentially, your child's science curriculum depends on the philosophy and resources of the school—and on the degree to which you are available to fill in the gaps.

How to Help with Science Homework

There's a good chance that your child will receive little or no science homework during elementary school. He may be asked to do some reading in his textbook and to answer questions at the end of the chapter. Or there may be a science workbook, like his social studies workbook, in which a short page is followed by reading comprehension questions.

If your school organizes an annual science fair, you may find yourself involved with your child in creating a major project for the fair. In a school with a solid science program that begins with hands-on work as early as the first grade, the science fair may be a natural development. But if your child has had very little experience with science, he may be justifiably overwhelmed by this big responsibility.

When your child has a big science project, follow the steps for handling a research project outlined above. Ideally, his teacher will help him select a topic, but if that doesn't happen, let your child look in the books listed below for ideas. He will probably need a variety of supplies, so make sure he plans exactly what he wants to do well in advance of the due date.

How to Help Your Child Learn about Science

Continue helping your child learn about science in these ways:

✎ **Don't take the commonplace for granted.** Talk about how the things in your house work. How does the refrigerator keep things cold? What makes the oven work? How does water get into the bathroom faucet?

✎ **Provide magnifying equipment.** Keep a magnifying glass in the house and use it to look at a host of objects up close. If your child seems interested you might also invest in a microscope and telescope.

✎ **Let your child take things apart.** Before you throw out an old appliance or piece of electronic equipment, give it to your child. Let him take it apart and see how it worked.

✎ **Reach for the stars.** If you live in a part of the world where you

The Science Fair Dilemma

The school science fair. Row upon row of tables heaped with students' science projects. At the front of the room, this year's winner: a full-scale, working model of a solar-powered electric car. Beside it, the beaming winner of the prize: Bobby Jones's dad.

To help or not to help: the school science fair brings the question to a head. If you don't help, your child carries through a complex project on her own, gaining a sense of mastery and success. If you do help, she has the chance to create a prizewinning project.

Science teachers Robert Bonnet and Tim Henson recently debated this subject. Here are some of their comments, as quoted in *NEA Today:*

Robert Bonnet (pro): "In the adult world, you get doors opened because someone goes to bat for you. Then you have to deliver, you have to make the opportunity work. Being in a similar situation can give a youngster a good lesson in showing initiative. . . . With ongoing guidance, a youngster can carry interest in a field of study beyond the school's requirements. Parents routinely support kids' efforts in sports, drama, music and art. Why not in an academic area?"

Tim Henson (con): "Our school district offered an elementary school science fair throughout most of the '80s. During that time . . . I watched the parents' competition against each other increase with each succeeding year. . . . [One year] a young lady presented a very elegant project that involved a good deal of woodworking. When I asked what part of the project was hers, she replied that while her dad had come up with the idea, drawn the plans, and cut and sanded and varnished the wood, she had pounded in some of the nails by herself!"

can see the night sky, by all means study it with your child. The moon is a good place to start, since you won't have any trouble identifying it. Watch the phases of the moon—your child might like to keep a calendar charting its progress. Next, begin to identify the planets and constellations.

✎ **Environmentalism begins at home.** When you talk to your child about the environment, you're bound to start thinking about the ways that you are helping or hurting the planet. If you don't already recycle, this is a good time to begin.

✎ **Make maps and a globe available.** If you have a globe in your living room, your child is likely to spend time poring over it. If you have room to post a map of the United States or the world somewhere in your home, your child will probably study that as well. Point out where your home is in relation to the rest of the country and the world. If you have relatives living in other states or countries, show your child where they live. Get a United States jigsaw puzzle.

Concentrate!

In order to study effectively, your child has to learn to concentrate. The more easily he is distracted, the harder it will be for him to concentrate. Some people concentrate better when they act out a small concentration ritual. Your child might want to take a few knee bends before sitting down, taking a deep breath and beginning. If he finds his attention wandering, he could repeat the ritual.

If your child has a great deal of trouble concentrating, it's possible that he has an attention disorder. See pp. 196–198. The suggestions on these pages will help any child learn to pay attention. Here are some other concentration techniques:

✎ **Breath counting.** Before he starts studying, ask your child to close his eyes and breathe in and out slowly and evenly. With each intake of breath he should think of a number—1, 2, 3, and so on. When he loses track, he should go back to the beginning and start again. Doing this exercise for three to five minutes will help focus his mind and minimize distractions.

✎ **Harness your energy.** Another approach is to harness the en-

Recommended Reading

Even if your child's science textbook leaves much to be desired, you can help him build a library of interesting science books. Some of these will help him come up with ideas for science projects, too.

The Way Things Work by David Macauley (Houghton Mifflin)

The Night Sky: A Guide for the Young Astronomer by Dennis Mammana (Running Press)

50 Simple Things Kids Can Do to Recycle by Earth Works Group (Green Leaf)

The Kids' Nature Book by Susan Milord (Williamson)

Science Express by Ontario Science Centre (Addison-Wesley)

Science Experiments You Can Eat by Vicki Cobb (Trophy)

Find the Constellations by H. A. Rey (Houghton Mifflin)

Mr. Wizard's Supermarket Science by Don Herbert (Random House)

The Reasons for Seasons by Linda Allison (Little, Brown)

For Kids Who Love Animals: A Guide to Sharing the Planet by Linda Koebner with the ASPCA (Living Planet Press)

Recommended Viewing

High quality science programming gives you an excuse to relax your rules about TV watching. Here are some worthwhile programs you could encourage your child to watch:

Nova

Cosmos

3–2–1 Contact

National Geographic specials

ergy that goes into being distracted. In the last chapter I mentioned that some children use music or rhythm to practice their spelling words. Let your child read over his homework aloud, possibly to a rhythmic or "rap" beat. If it helps him to tap his feet or slap the table while he works, that's fine. This kind of behavior sometimes looks like goofing off when it isn't. (Of course, it sometimes *is* goofing off, so make sure your child is boogieing down to the tune of his homework, not to some other interior voice.)

Put Your Thinking Cap On

As your child's brain develops, he is ready for increasingly complex mental processes. Here are some word games that will help build his thinking skills. All these games are great for car trips, long walks, or waiting in line.

Twenty Questions

Here's how you play: One player thinks of a person. The second person asks yes-or-no questions: Is it a man? Is he alive? Do I know him? Is he a politician? And so on. Keep track of the number of questions asked: the guesser only has twenty chances to arrive at the right answer.

A more challenging variation of this game is called Botticelli. One player thinks of a person—let's say Ulysses S. Grant. He gives the first initial of the person's last name, in this case G. The second player thinks of someone whose last name begins with that letter and forms a question like this: "Are you a major league pitcher?" To which the first player answers, if he can think of a specific name, "No, I'm not Dwight Gooden." If he can't think of an appropriate name, the second player gets to ask a yes-or-no question. The first player tries to evade the second player by coming up with alternative responses. For example, when asked "Are you a head of state?" he might answer, "No, I'm not Mikhail Gorbachev," even though the name he's thinking of (Ulysses S. Grant) was in fact a head of state.

Milly Tilly

Here's a game that will drive your child (and any adults you try it on) crazy. Milly Tilly likes cheese but she doesn't like milk. She likes Beethoven but she doesn't like Brahms. Milly Tilly likes dinner but she doesn't like breakfast. She likes school but she doesn't like homework. How does Milly Tilly decide? The answer seems obvious once you get it but it's surprisingly hard to figure out. Milly Tilly's name is a clue: she only likes words with double letters. Once your child gets the system, he'll have a great time trying it on his friends.

Rhyme Time

What would you call a distant automobile? A far car. A hilarious rabbit? A funny bunny. A criminal cantaloupe? A melon felon. That's how you play Rhyme Time, a deceptively simple game in which one player comes up with wacky definitions and the others have to identify the rhyming solutions. The game builds critical thinking skills and is lots of fun too.

Conundrums

"A man, wearing a backpack, lies dead in the desert." This is the single sentence that introduces a famous conundrum. The guessers have to come up with yes-or-no questions (Did he die of thirst? Does it matter that he's in the desert? Was there food in the backpack?) to find out what happened. The solution in this case is that the man jumped out of a plane and his parachute (which was in the backpack) failed to open. Another good conundrum: "If she hadn't seen the light, she wouldn't have died." ("She" turns out to be a moth.) A good conundrum can take hours to solve (the entire drive from Big Sur to Los Angeles, for example).

Special Cases

I hope that what you've read so far has given you an arsenal of strategies and ideas for ways to ease the strain of homework time at your house. Ideally, each person who reads this book will come away with a different game plan, one that is tailored to her particular child's situation and personality.

Each household has its own unique circumstances that affect the homework dynamic. At my house, a demanding new baby came along just as my daughter needed more supervision with her homework. My friend Marsha's son Henry is active in so many sports that getting his homework done is becoming a problem. My friends Tom and Fran are divorced; their kids carry homework back and forth between two households.

The following pages address particular circumstances that may be affecting homework in your house. Use the suggestions and strategies described here to supplement the ideas you've gotten from the rest of the book.

When You're Not There

Do you really need to be with your child when she is doing her homework? Probably not. Many teachers allow children time to work on homework in the classroom, and that practice usually works out just fine. If you are not home in the afternoons, you may want to arrange for your child to complete some or all of her homework before you come home for the evening. That way, you'll both have more time for enjoyable pursuits.

If homework is a source of strain in your family, arranging for your child to do homework under someone else's guidance may actually be a good solution. Make sure, however, that your child is in a situation where she'll get the support she needs. Here are some possible approaches:

✎ **After-school programs.** Increasingly, after-school programs—whether in school or away from school—are providing opportunities for children to do their homework. Michelle Seligson, director of the School-Age Childcare Project at Wellesley College, says, "I used to be opposed to children doing homework in their after-school programs because of the tendency of some programs to turn after-school into an extended school day. But I've changed my mind because parents and children are both expressing the need for homework to be accomplished during after-school."

Seligson says that doing homework should be an option that parents and children select, not a requirement of attending an after-school program. Furthermore, parents should make sure that the people who staff the after-school program (who may not be teachers) are qualified to supervise homework and that the program provides a quiet, appropriate place for children to work.

✎ **Babysitters.** If your child comes home to a babysitter after school, you may want to ask the babysitter to supervise the homework process. Again, make sure your babysitter is someone you believe can supervise effectively. She should be a bright, well-educated person who can support your child without taking over and doing the homework for her. A teenager who does well in school may be able to assume this role—in fact, your child may really respond well to someone this age. Or try the student placement office at your local college or university. You may be lucky enough to find an education major who will value this opportunity to work with your child.

Consider hiring a male high school or college student for this job. While male full-time childcare workers are hard to find, part-time care-givers come in both genders. Particularly if your child is a boy, this older role model may provide inspiration.

Joan Friedman, who runs a babysitting service called A Choice Nanny in New York City, places college students in part-time after-school positions. She points out that when you're hiring someone to supervise homework while you're away, you're also hiring someone to look after your child. You want a loving care-giver as well as a competent homework supervisor. She suggests asking prospective after-school care-givers these questions:

1. Why are you interested in this job?
2. What kinds of child care experience do you have?
3. What are your own educational goals?
4. How does taking care of my child fit into your future plans?

"When Matt started elementary school, I let Wendy, the nice, grandmotherly woman who had always looked after him, continue as our housekeeper. But as his homework became more demanding, I began to see that Wendy wasn't really great at helping Matt. She was so wonderful in other ways that I didn't mind, I just had him do his homework at night.

"But when Wendy retired, I hired a college student as his after-school care-giver. She's really tuned in to his homework and I can talk with her about how to handle any problems that come up. Now his homework is done when I come home from work and we have time to do fun stuff together."

—LINDA K.

✎ **Libraries.** Around the country, libraries are beginning to become involved in after-school care. In some cases, this involvement is born of necessity: Many working parents send their children to the library after school in the hope that they'll receive free, safe after-school care. Although this is a common practice, it is not an appropriate way to use the library. Only a child who is old enough for self-care should be sent to the library on her own, unless she is attending a special library program.

One such program is Seattle's SPLASH, the Seattle Public Library After-School Happenings program. Children's librarians and parent volunteers collaborate in a program that begins with a half-hour of supervised quiet time in which children may read or do homework. The rest of the time is devoted to activities.

You may want to contact your local library and find out if a similar program is available. If you have determined that your child is ready for self-care, talk with your children's librarian and find out whether she'd be available for questions if your child chooses to do her homework at the library.

If your child does her homework when you're not around and she is doing well in school, you probably don't need to go over her homework on a daily basis. Do check in with her at least once a week to find out what is going on. In some cases, you may need to be involved on a daily basis. Perhaps your child can do some of her homework when you're apart and then work with you on hard problems or particular subjects that are causing difficulty.

Divorce and Joint Custody

When a family goes through a divorce, everyone is affected. Your child's schoolwork is likely to suffer temporarily while she's experiencing the shock and confusion of radical change. Later on, you'll need new approaches for dealing with homework as a single parent. If you share custody with your former spouse, you'll need to find ways to ensure that homework isn't disrupted.

Joan Anderson, author of *The Single Mother's Book* (Peachtree), comments: "School performance is affected by divorce; children's grades and their self-esteem will take a dive at the time of the divorce." It's important that single parents recognize this fact, Anderson says, so that they realize that although school problems may result from the divorce they do not necessarily result from poor homework supervision at home. Instead of blaming yourself or your spouse (or letting your ex-spouse blame you) for your child's school problems, you may need to accept these problems as an unfortunate but temporary side effect of the divorce.

Make sure that homework is a structured part of your child's day. Anderson recommends, "Set aside an hour of quiet time, when you sit down too. Read a book or listen to quiet music while your children study." If homework was going fairly smoothly before the divorce, try to provide continuity by ensuring that the same rules and conditions apply. If homework has always been a problem, sit down with your child and map out a new approach.

Neil Kalter, author of the very useful book *Growing Up with Divorce* (Fawcett), identifies several distress reactions that may occur among elementary school–age children: sadness, depression, anger, anxiety, fear, somatic complaints, and general withdrawal. It's easy to see that when a child experiences frightening reactions like these, daily activities, including homework, are bound to be affected. As you help your child work through the pain and trauma of the divorce, homework problems should begin to ease up.

"**M**y approach to joint custody is to let the teacher know what my situation is and rely on her help. Over the years, the teachers have come to understand that I am the one who remembers things. The kids are with me at the end of the week, so when the teacher has an important notice, she sends it home then. I can't coordinate with my ex-husband because he isn't interested so I coordinate with the teacher.

"When a problem arises, my ex-husband, Frank, and I go together to a conference with the teacher. Frank's live-in companion has also gone to these conferences so that the three adults who are involved can meet with the teacher and talk things over together. My relationship with my ex-husband is contentious most of the time so it's best if we go to the teacher and he hears the teacher say what needs to be done. That way *I'm* not saying he has to do this or that.

"Also, I happen to believe that doing their homework is my children's responsibility. I try not to argue with them or my ex-husband about what is or isn't done at his house. That's not my responsibility."

—BETTY W.

Joint custody can be a blessing for both children and parents but it also provides unique challenges. How can your child complete a week-long project when she lives in two different households? What do you do when she leaves an important book at the other parent's home? Here are some ways of handling joint custody:

✎ **If you have a good relationship with your ex, map out a joint homework strategy.** Joint custody works best when parents can communicate openly and work together for the child's good. Establishing similar homework policies in both households will certainly increase your child's sense of security and continuity. Here's how one set of parents share responsibility for their child's homework: "Sophie gets two sets of weekly homework, spelling and math," says Ann P. "I work on the spelling with her when I have her early in the week. Her dad works on the math homework, which he's really good at. Even though the spelling isn't due until Friday, I try to make sure she has most of the work done before she goes to his house. Otherwise, she'll have to do it all with him and that's not fair." If one of you is better at supervising a particular subject than the other, by all means divide up the homework that way if you can.

✎ **Enlist the teacher as your ally.** Early in the year, explain your situation to your child's teacher. She may be willing to set up a joint conference at which you can all discuss ways of facilitating homework. Turning to the teacher for advice can be a way to avoid conflict between parents.

✎ **Accept the fact that you are sharing responsibility for homework.** Your standards may be different from those of your ex-spouse. It can be very frustrating to discover that your child got a low mark on her spelling test because she was up watching videos with Dad instead of studying her spelling words. But that is between your child and your ex-spouse. You can't take complete responsibility for your child's homework, and you can't control what happens at your ex-spouse's home.

✎ **Buy a small assignment book and make sure your child carries it back and forth from one house to the other.** Ask your child to write down all her assignments in this notebook. You and your former spouse might write notes to each other in this notebook: "Jenny finished the first draft of her essay; still needs to edit and rewrite." If she has time, the teacher may be willing to write comments in the notebook too.

✎ **Consider rearranging your joint custody schedule.** When your child was smaller, three days at one house followed by four at the other may have made a lot of sense. But if her homework is based on a week-long schedule, it may be easier to alternate homes every week. Your child is probably old enough to handle week-long separations at this point.

✎ **Consider having duplicate books at each house.** Leaving a schoolbook behind at one parent's home is a typical problem with joint custody. If this happens frequently it may be worthwhile to ask yourselves why it is happening so often. Is the child unconsciously choosing to leave a part of herself behind? Or arranging to see the other parent again before the appointed time? If so, you may need to talk with your child more about her feelings about the divorce. Different families handle the left-behind book issue differently. Some parents feel that by facing the consequences, the child learns to be more responsible. Others feel that helping the child retrieve the missing book is the kindest approach. Still others circumvent the problem by buying or borrowing from the school an extra set of books to keep at the second parent's home.

Learning Problems

As recently as our own childhoods, the kid who had trouble reading or who found math extremely difficult was often labeled "slow" and left to sink or swim on her own. These days, if your child is having trouble in school it has probably already occurred to you to ask whether she might have a learning problem.

If you are having difficulty with your child over homework, especially if the homework seems to be taking too long or seems to be very hard for your child, consider the possibility that your child may have a learning disability. Undiagnosed, a learning problem can look like laziness, stupidity, or contrariness. Diagnosed and treated, many learning problems can be overcome.

There is no single set of symptoms that add up to a learning problem. In the most general terms, a learning disability is a disorder in the process of using spoken or written language. Learning disorders can affect a child's manner of listening, thinking, reading, writing, spelling and/or performing mathematical computations.

There is considerable debate among educators over how to diagnose and treat learning disabilities. Most acknowledge the existence of these kinds of problems but many feel the label "learning disabled" has been overused.

If you suspect that your child may have a learning disability, ask the school to conduct an evaluation. According to the Education of All Handicapped Children Act, passed in 1975, every public school is required to conduct a complete psychological and educational evaluation of children suspected of having learning disabilities. Based on this evaluation, the school is required to meet with parents and outline an Individualized Education Plan (IEP), which will be tailored to meet the child's particular needs. The plan may involve special education classes designed to complement the child's classroom education.

If you are not satisfied with the results of the school's evaluation, you may want to initiate your own investigation. Consult your local university to find the name of a qualified psychologist. You may want to consider paying for special tutoring or enrolling your child in a special school.

Although it may be hard for you to accept the fact that your child has a learning disability, it can also be a tremendous relief to realize that there is a biological reason for her difficulties at school. And homework should become easier when you receive guidance and counseling from your child's special education teacher.

Pamela Reiss is a learning disability specialist at Mount Sinai Hospital in New York City. She offers these suggestions for parents who are supervising their learning-disabled children's homework:

✎ **When appropriate, read aloud to your child.** It may not be appropriate to read your child's reading assignment to her, but it can be very helpful to read aloud homework assignment directions, social studies and science texts, and other written material. This way your child can concentrate on the content of the reading instead of struggling to decode the words. If you're not available to read aloud, perhaps an older sibling or an adult friend can read aloud to her.

✎ **Find out about the learning strategies that work for your child.** Your child's special education teacher probably has certain techniques that help your child learn. Find out what these are so you can use them at home. For example, if the special education teacher uses manipulatives to teach your child math, try to have the same kind of manipulatives at home.

✎ **Make your child's teacher your ally.** Ideally, your child's special education teacher will work with her regular teacher to tailor assignments to your child's abilities. You should communicate regularly with your child's teacher too. As your child's advocate, ask the teacher to give her shorter, more manageable assignments. If spelling is a problem for your child, maybe the teacher can overlook spelling errors in essays and other written assignments. Or she may be willing to give two grades, one for content and one for overall neatness. Perhaps the teacher will allow your child to hand in tape-recorded answers to her homework instead of written answers. Also, she may be willing to give your child oral instead of written tests.

"Our seven-year-old, Erica, has been diagnosed as having a speech and language disorder. She has trouble processing information and taking it in. The less distraction and stimulation she has, the better.

"We work on her homework on the floor of our dining room. It's a sparsely furnished room with a hardwood floor and good light. We sit on the floor together while Erica works. By getting down on the floor with her, I'm on her level and we get good eye contact. She concentrates there much better than she does sitting at a desk or a table.

"Sometimes I give her a bowl of Cheerios to eat while she works. Children with this particular problem respond well when they have something to do with their hands. We also have a tiddlywinks game, and whenever Erica gets an answer right, I put a chip in the pot; that shows her the progress she's making. I'm really delighted with the way she persists and gets the work done."

—SARA H.

For Further Information

For more information on learning disabilities, contact:

Learning Disabilities Association
4156 Library Road
Pittsburgh, PA 15234

Hyperactivity and Attention Deficit Disorder

Hyperactivity and attention deficit disorder are conditions that are often associated with learning disabilities. Not every child who is learning-disabled has one of these conditions, nor does every child with one of these conditions also have a learning disability. But many children have both learning disabilities and attention problems.

Children with these disorders are easily distracted. It is hard for them to sustain interest in a given text or other object of attention. They also find it difficult to consciously shift their attention from one subject to another without losing information and to hold more than one thing in mind at once.

Margaret Jo Shepherd, director of the Learning Disabilities Program at Teachers College, Columbia University, has worked extensively with children who have attention disorders. In her clinical work, Dr. Shepherd uses these approaches to help children with ADD and other disorders become more attentive:

✏ **Help children read selectively by thinking about the text ahead of time.** Dr. Shepherd asks students to brainstorm with themselves before they begin reading. They should ask themselves what they know about a topic before they begin reading. This way, they can bring existing knowledge to bear on the new task. They should also ask themselves questions as they read (for example, "Who's the main character?"). This will help them stay focused.

✎ **Teach children how to summarize.** Dr. Shepherd shows her students how to construct a summary that identifies the main idea of the text and eliminates anything trivial or redundant. The experience of summarizing trains students to focus their attention on pertinent information.

✎ **Teach children to be organized.** All children work best when they are organized, but this is especially true of children who have ADD. They need to know exactly what they have to do and to have all the materials and equipment they need to carry out their tasks.

✎ **Teach children to pay attention to whether they are paying attention.** Dr. Shepherd helps children to think about the act of paying attention. She asks them to talk about times when they did or didn't pay attention. Sometimes she sets a timer for seven or ten minutes and asks the child to notice, when it goes off, whether she's still paying attention to her original task.

✎ **Let them talk to themselves.** Dr. Shepherd has children describe to themselves what they're supposed to do. For example, if they're writing a paragraph they talk it through to themselves before starting to write.

If you suspect your child is hyperactive or has a greater-than-usual problem with paying attention, you might want to read a very useful book, *If Your Child Is Hyperactive, Inattentive, Impulsive, Distractible . . .: Helping the ADD (Attention Deficit Disorder)/Hyperactive Child*, by Stephen W. Garber, Marianne Daniels Garber, and Robyn Freedman Spizman (Villard).

Children with these conditions have special needs when it comes to doing homework, says Marianne Daniels Garber. These are some of the suggestions she gives to parents of her patients:

✎ **Provide lots of structure.** "These kids don't handle unstructured time well, they're not self-starters," Garber comments. "They do better knowing the rules and keeping to a very specific schedule." For these children, a set homework time every night is probably a better idea than a homework schedule that varies from day to day.

✎ **Teach your child to check herself.** "Carelessness can be a problem," says Garber. "Teach your child to check her own work. On the other hand, don't make her feel that it has to be perfect all the time." Help your child find the middle ground between carelessness and perfectionism.

✎ **Teach your child to remember.** Garber recommends a body-scan method. Have your child mentally look over her body and think: "Do I have everything? What am I missing?"

✎ **Make changes gradually.** "You can't make a child shape up overnight," Garber comments. "Instead, focus on the most glaring problem. For example, let's say you have a child who won't stay in her seat. Start by asking her to sit in her seat for thirty seconds. The next day have her sit for a minute and so on. Reward positive behavior."

For Further Information

For more information on hyperactivity and ADD, contact:

Children with Attention Deficit Disorders
1859 Birth Pine Island Road
Suite 185
Plantation, FL 33322

Gifted Children

Like the label "learning-disabled," the label "gifted" is open to debate. Giftedness is usually identified by IQ testing, a process that may or may not reflect children's real intelligence. IQ testing also tests only one aspect of giftedness—intelligence—and fails to reveal artistic and other gifts.

Nevertheless, if your child has been designated gifted, you may want to let her take advantage of special gifted programs in your school district. Unlike with learning disabilities, there is no federally mandated program to help the gifted. However, many states and individual school districts offer special programs that may enrich your child's education.

If your child is gifted, she may find her regular classroom education—and her homework—uninspiring and even dull. A gifted child, left to languish in a middle-of-the-road class, may form the mistaken impression that education is a tiresome waste of time. Try to counterbalance that impression by offering exciting, interesting educational opportunities at home.

The extra activities suggested throughout this book will be particularly helpful to the gifted child. Take your gifted child to museums and nature centers and theatrical performances. Do science experiments together, tackle challenging math problems, and find books for her that are at her reading level. The gifted child will probably crave information, and the more you can provide the better. But don't turn your gifted child into a hothouse flower. Follow her lead—she'll tell you when she's had enough.

"I don't like to use the word 'gifted,' although I certainly believe my daughter is bright and that the school doesn't challenge her sufficiently. Whenever I complain that the teacher isn't giving enough homework, I find that Julia is doing her homework in half the time it takes the other kids to complete theirs.

"I try not to get overly involved in Julia's education, but I also try to fill in the gaps when they are really glaring. For example, she was given an assignment to do a report on Prince Edward Island. But there's nothing to learn about Prince Edward Island. It was a waste of time for her to spend six months on this subject. So instead we read all the *Anne of Green Gables* books together and then we saw the movie. Then we got out a map of Prince Edward Island and we looked up all the places that appear in the books.

"Even though Julia is in the ninety-ninth percentile in her class, I feel that she isn't getting enough stimulation in school. So to me the important thing is that we have an environment at home that stimulates learning. For example, when I realized that Julia wasn't learning how to express herself clearly in writing, I just supplemented what was happening in school. I had her write me a two-page letter on any subject every week. She loved doing it and it helped her form coherent thoughts on paper.

"In a way, we've had to create a fragile balance: Julia can be one child at school and have this secret life of learning at home. But this is exactly the way I was brought up too, and I think it works."

—MOLLY F.

For Further Information

For more information on programs for gifted children, write to:

Program for the Education of the Gifted and Talented
U.S. Department of Education
400 Maryland Avenue, S.W.
Washington, D.C. 20202

When Your Child Has a Long Absence from School

When your child is absent from school for more than a few days, she may fall behind in her schoolwork. If she's not too sick, it's a good idea to visit the school and bring home her homework as well as classwork that she can handle at home.

Don't assume that your child's teacher will get in touch with you or send work home with a neighboring child. Get in touch with the teacher yourself and ask her to compile some work for her to do at home.

If your child is too ill to do work at home, you'll have to wait until she gets better. When she's well enough to start school, though, you may need to work with her to bring her skills up to the level of the class.

If your child misses several months of school, consider letting her repeat her present grade next year. This can be a hard decision to make, but in many cases it saves your child from falling permanently behind.

"When my son was in second grade, he had a bone infection and he was out of school for six months. Once he was in the hospital, it was hard to keep up with the schoolwork. So when he got out we held him back a year and had him repeat second grade. The decision has really worked out. Now he's a happy, outgoing twelve-year-old. I feel he's more mature than his classmates, not just in the sense of being a year older but also in the way he's so independent and so sure of himself. If we had made him keep up with his first class, he would still be struggling. Holding him back made a world of difference."

—DONNA J.

Appendix

Software Companies

Britannica Software
345 4th Street
San Francisco, CA 94107
800-572-2272

Broderbund Software
17 Paul Drive
San Rafael, CA 94913
800-521-6263

Davidson and Associates, Inc.
3135 Kashiwa Street
Torrance, CA 90505
800-556-6141

DLM Software
One DLM Park
Allen, TX 75002
800-527-4747

The Learning Company
6493 Kaiser Drive
Fremont, CA 94555
800-852-2255

Scholastic Family Software
P.O. Box 7502
Jefferson City, MO 65102
800-541-5513

Sunburst Communications
101 Castleton Street
Pleasantville, NY 10570
800-628-8897

Weekly Reader Software
10 Station Place
Norfolk, CT 06058
800-327-1473